Immanuel Kant

Titles in the series Critical Lives present the work of leading cultural figures of the modern period. Each book explores the life of the artist, writer, philosopher or architect in question and relates it to their major works.

In the same series

Hannah Arendt *Samantha Rose Hill*
Antonin Artaud *David A. Shafer*
John Ashbery *Jess Cotton*
Roland Barthes *Andy Stafford*
Georges Bataille *Stuart Kendall*
Charles Baudelaire *Rosemary Lloyd*
Jean Baudrillard *Emmanuelle Fantin and Bran Nicol*
Simone de Beauvoir *Ursula Tidd*
Samuel Beckett *Andrew Gibson*
Walter Benjamin *Esther Leslie*
John Berger *Andy Merrifield*
Leonard Bernstein *Paul R. Laird*
Joseph Beuys *Claudia Mesch*
Jorge Luis Borges *Jason Wilson*
Johannes Brahms *John Worthen*
Constantin Brancusi *Sanda Miller*
Bertolt Brecht *Philip Glahn*
Charles Bukowski *David Stephen Calonne*
Mikhail Bulgakov *J.A.E. Curtis*
William S. Burroughs *Phil Baker*
Byron *David Ellis*
John Cage *Rob Haskins*
Albert Camus *Edward J. Hughes*
Fidel Castro *Nick Caistor*
Paul Cézanne *Jon Kear*
Coco Chanel *Linda Simon*
Noam Chomsky *Wolfgang B. Sperlich*
John Clare *Sarah Houghton-Walker*
Jean Cocteau *James S. Williams*
Colette *Kathleen Antonioli*
Joseph Conrad *Robert Hampson*
H.D. (Hilda Doolittle) *Lara Vetter*
Salvador Dalí *Mary Ann Caws*
Charles Darwin *J. David Archibald*
Guy Debord *Andy Merrifield*
Claude Debussy *David J. Code*
Gilles Deleuze *Frida Beckman*
Fyodor Dostoevsky *Robert Bird*
Marcel Duchamp *Caroline Cros*
Sergei Eisenstein *Mike O'Mahony*
Frantz Fanon *James S. Williams*
William Faulkner *Kirk Curnutt*
Gustave Flaubert *Anne Green*
Ford Madox Ford *Max Saunders*
Michel Foucault *David Macey*
Benjamin Franklin *Kevin J. Hayes*
Sigmund Freud *Matthew ffytche*
Mahatma Gandhi *Douglas Allen*
Antoni Gaudí *Michael Eaude*
Jean Genet *Stephen Barber*
Allen Ginsberg *Steve Finbow*
Johann Wolfgang von Goethe *Jeremy Adler*
Günter Grass *Julian Preece*
Ernest Hemingway *Verna Kale*
E.T.A. Hoffmann *Ritchie Robertson*
Langston Hughes *W. Jason Miller*
Victor Hugo *Bradley Stephens*
Zora Neale Hurston *Cheryl R. Hopson*
Aldous Huxley *Jake Poller*
J.-K. Huysmans *Ruth Antosh*
Christopher Isherwood *Jake Poller*
Derek Jarman *Michael Charlesworth*
Alfred Jarry *Jill Fell*
James Joyce *Andrew Gibson*
Carl Jung *Paul Bishop*
Franz Kafka *Sander L. Gilman*
Frida Kahlo *Gannit Ankori*
Immanuel Kant *Robert Wicks*
Søren Kierkegaard *Alastair Hannay*
Yves Klein *Nuit Banai*
Arthur Koestler *Edward Saunders*
Akira Kurosawa *Peter Wild*
D. H. Lawrence *David Ellis*
Lenin *Lars T. Lih*
Jack London *Kenneth K. Brandt*
Pierre Loti *Richard M. Berrong*
Rosa Luxemburg *Dana Mills*
Jean-François Lyotard *Kiff Bamford*
René Magritte *Patricia Allmer*
Gustav Mahler *Stephen Downes*
Stéphane Mallarmé *Roger Pearson*
Thomas Mann *Herbert Lehnert and Eva Wessell*
Gabriel García Márquez *Stephen M. Hart*
Karl Marx *Paul Thomas*
Henri Matisse *Kathryn Brown*
Guy de Maupassant *Christopher Lloyd*
Herman Melville *Kevin J. Hayes*
Henry Miller *David Stephen Calonne*
Yukio Mishima *Damian Flanagan*
Eadweard Muybridge *Marta Braun*
Vladimir Nabokov *Barbara Wyllie*
Pablo Neruda *Dominic Moran*
Friedrich Nietzsche *Ritchie Robertson*
Georgia O'Keeffe *Nancy J. Scott*
Richard Owen *Patrick Armstrong*
Octavio Paz *Nick Caistor*
Fernando Pessoa *Bartholomew Ryan*
Pablo Picasso *Mary Ann Caws*
Edgar Allan Poe *Kevin J. Hayes*
Ezra Pound *Alec Marsh*
Sergei Prokofiev *Christina Guillaumier*
Marcel Proust *Adam Watt*
Sergei Rachmaninoff *Rebecca Mitchell*
Maurice Ravel *Emily Kilpatrick*
Arthur Rimbaud *Seth Whidden*
John Ruskin *Andrew Ballantyne*
Jean-Paul Sartre *Andrew Leak*
Erik Satie *Mary E. Davis*
Arnold Schoenberg *Mark Berry*
Arthur Schopenhauer *Peter B. Lewis*
Dmitry Shostakovich *Pauline Fairclough*
Adam Smith *Jonathan Conlin*
Susan Sontag *Jerome Boyd Maunsell*
Gertrude Stein *Lucy Daniel*
Stendhal *Francesco Manzini*
Robert Louis Stevenson *Glenda Norquay*
Igor Stravinsky *Jonathan Cross*
Rabindranath Tagore *Bashabi Fraser*
Pyotr Tchaikovsky *Philip Ross Bullock*
Dylan Thomas *John Goodby and Chris Wigginton*
Leo Tolstoy *Andrei Zorin*
Leon Trotsky *Paul Le Blanc*
Mark Twain *Kevin J. Hayes*
Pauline Viardot *Natasha Loges*
Richard Wagner *Raymond Furness*
Alfred Russel Wallace *Patrick Armstrong*
Simone Weil *Palle Yourgrau*
Tennessee Williams *Paul Ibell*
Ludwig Wittgenstein *Edward Kanterian*
Virginia Woolf *Ira Nadel*
Frank Lloyd Wright *Robert McCarter*

Immanuel Kant

Robert Wicks

REAKTION BOOKS

To those who share Kant's peaceful vision of a rationally unified world

Published by Reaktion Books Ltd
2–4 Sebastian Street
London EC1V 0HE, UK

www.reaktionbooks.co.uk

First published 2026

EU GPSR Authorised Representative
Logos Europe, 9 rue Nicolas Poussin, 17000, La Rochelle, France
email: contact@logoseurope.eu

Printed and bound in Great Britain by Bell & Bain, Glasgow

A catalogue record for this book is available from the British Library

ISBN 978 1 83639 251 4

Contents

Friedrich Hagemann, *Immanuel Kant*, 1801, marble bust.

Introduction

In most people's minds, not much is known about the life of Immanuel Kant, one of the most influential philosophers in the history of philosophy. Common knowledge is usually limited to how he lived almost his entire life in Königsberg, a city at the remote edge of the Prussian empire, never travelling far from home, or the anecdote that his neighbourhood residents could set their watches by noting when he passed by each day on his precisely scheduled walks. The latter, as is easily imagined, is usually accompanied by mild amusement and the assumption that Kant led an uninteresting academic life and was probably an eccentric.

It is a pity that such a biography-discouraging image has prevailed, distracting us as it does from appreciating Kant's admirable personal qualities and the unexpected aspects of his life, such as his gregariousness and his friendships with army generals, civic leaders and admirers from the nobility of Königsberg. Here, for years, he enjoyed a permanent invitation to dine at the table of one of the most powerful families in the city.

The source of the more popularly encountered image of Kant can be traced to an 1835 essay by the German poet Heinrich Heine (1797–1856), who did not know Kant personally:

> Immanuel Kant's life story is difficult to describe, because he had neither a life nor a story. He lived a mechanically ordered, almost abstract bachelor existence in a quiet isolated lane in Königsberg, an old city on the north-eastern border of Germany. In my opinion, not even the great cathedral clock there went

about its daily labor with less passion and more regularity than its compatriot Immanuel Kant. Getting up, drinking coffee, writing, giving lectures, eating, walking: everything had its set time, and the neighbors knew that it was exactly half past three when Immanuel Kant, in his grey frock-coat, rattan cane in hand, emerged from his front door and strolled in the direction of small Lindenallee, which is still called 'Philosopher's Way' on his account.[1]

To be sure, Kant's life was neither as amazingly adventurous as those of Alexander, Julius Caesar and Napoleon, nor as eventful as those of Benjamin Franklin, Abraham Lincoln and Mahatma Gandhi. Kant worked almost exclusively in the realm of ideas and his impact on the world has come to us quietly through his books and other writings. In this respect, he impressed some of the greatest minds of the age, such as Johann Wolfgang von Goethe (1749–1832), who, as Arthur Schopenhauer reported, 'once said to me that when he read a page of Kant he felt as though he had entered a bright room'.[2]

A highlight of this biography is Kant's inspiring personality: he embodied extreme intellectual ambition, extraordinary willpower and self-discipline, had astonishing conversational abilities, was intelligently attentive to his physical constitution, and integrated these talents into a single-minded dedication to the moral education of humanity, exemplified in both his classroom teaching and his writings. By examining his life, useful and memorable models of conduct emerge for organizing one's own. Born with a frail, slightly deformed body, he lived to the ripe age of almost eighty in a century when the science of medicine was not as advanced as it is today, not because he was lucky, but because he took close care of himself in the most determined and meticulous way. His daily walks were not those of an eccentric, but of someone who thought carefully about his physical condition and had developed an informed medical awareness.

Aside from the small circle of contemporary Kant scholars, it is virtually unknown that Kant wrote mainly about physical science in his early years and conceived of himself as being in the same intellectual league as Isaac Newton. His writings from that time match those of professors of physics rather than philosophy. And this was not mere appearance: his abilities were genuine. Kant's nebular hypothesis about the origin of the heavenly bodies is still respected and accepted. He wrote with implicitly philosophical concerns from the start, even in what appear to be purely scientific works, but as the years went on this philosophical dimension became more pronounced, coincident with his increasing moral concern for the future of humanity. Although the power of his intellect did not diminish until he was much older, Kant's personality changed as he acquired a greater sense of humility. His extensive written correspondence with others makes it evident that he was well loved as a teacher and highly respected as a scholar and human being.

It is true enough that Kant is usually understood as a representative of Enlightenment-style thinking from the Age of Reason. He published his groundbreaking *Critique of Pure Reason* in 1781 as the Enlightenment spirit was waning, however, and intellectual fashion was moving away from an unquestioning commitment to reason as the final court of appeal with respect to the great questions and its accompanying 'world-as-a-mechanical-clockwork' analogy. As someone standing on the threshold of a new era, Kant struggled in the later part of his academic life to resist the emerging style of thinking – a style, to his dismay, represented by one of his best students – that would soon define the nineteenth century, where mechanical models were replaced with images expressive of life, organic unity, instinct and the unconscious.

In what follows we will explore the times in which Kant lived, his Pietistic upbringing and its long-term influence on his thought, the initial frustrations in his search for intellectual fame, his experiences under the rule of four different Prussian kings – some of whom were liberating, some of whom were oppressive – his reactions to momentous historical events such as the French Revolution, his unshakable theism and social optimism, and his extensive socializing and friendships, which included some of the most prominent people in the city.

Kant was a person of ideas, so a separate chapter will be devoted to presenting the main themes in his famous three *Critiques*. In the concluding chapters, we will consider critically some of the accusations made against Kant – namely, that he was a sexist, antisemite and racist – after which we will describe his final years, marked initially by the loss of sight in one of his eyes, followed by a gradual, heartbreaking decline in his memory and health.

Some of the interpretations of these aspects of Kant's life will differ noticeably from other biographies, in particular the influence of Pietism on his thought. Some minimize or deny this influence, but to this interpreter it seems to be evident, despite how Kant's philosophical outlook was straightforwardly hostile to some of Pietism's definitive features such as its emotionalism and doctrinal rigidity. Similarly, the influence of the mystic Emanuel Swedenborg is often overlooked or downplayed, but there is reason to acknowledge his strong impact on Kant. To conclude, we will describe some of the enduring influence Kant's ideas have had on the history of philosophy and culture.

Heinrich Heine wrote that Kant had neither a life nor a story, blind to how greatness of character can display itself unobtrusively with a centuries-long impact. This also, unfortunately, has been the stubborn influence of his remark on the popular image of Kant. Perhaps, as appreciation grows for the details of Kant's life, this less informed caricature will find its proper place as a minor historical note and a mere trace of the past.

1

Königsberg and the World Scene in the 1700s

Although time travel is often thought of as a science-fiction fantasy or hope for the future, it has been possible for centuries. Travelling by ship, aeroplane, car or even walking across certain national borders, moving from one society to another, can be akin to travelling to another era. Suppose one is visiting a mountain village with mud dwellings and no electricity, where the flour to make bread is ground manually between two large stones, where charcoal stoves are used to cook food and where travel is by donkey rather than motor vehicle. Upon returning on a flight to a modern city, it can feel as if one were on a spaceship into the future. The clocks might show the same time in Munich and in the Atlas Mountains, but the difference in cultural time is a matter of centuries.

Just as these experiences are possible today, so it was in the 1700s when Immanuel Kant was living. Captain James Cook (1728–1779), one of Kant's close contemporaries, landed in New Zealand in October 1769 to encounter the Māori tribal culture – a group whom the British stunned and subdued with their formidable ships and weapons. It was a startling contrast, perhaps comparable to how a UFO landing would appear to us. The cultural gap is equally implicit in a joke that Kant recited in his *Critique of the Power of Judgment* (§54) about an Englishman living in India, north of Mumbai, and his local guest. When the Englishman opened a beer bottle, the guest laughed and laughed as the foam spewed out. When asked what was so funny, the man said that the foam spewing out was understandable enough, but it was incomprehensible how one could get the foam into the bottle to begin with!

As is true for our present world, the 1700s comprised a patchwork of societies whose practices embodied the realities of different phases of cultural development. Some people were still living according to traditions that had remained virtually unchanged for centuries. Others lived in a more technologically advanced world. On the European scene, the Industrial Revolution began in Great Britain in the late eighteenth century, but in the German-speaking areas it did not become manifest until decades thereafter. Political and philosophical ideas that challenged the authority of hereditary monarchies became influential in France and North America in the 1700s, helping to spark two world-historical revolutions, but those ideas were slow to have a comparable impact upon other nations and continents. Indeed, traditions tend to change only sluggishly: even today in Europe, there are hereditary monarchies in the United Kingdom, Spain, Sweden, the Netherlands, Norway, Monaco, Luxembourg, Liechtenstein, Denmark and Belgium.

In 1781 Kant published his most influential book, the *Critique of Pure Reason*. To set this book's appearance in a wider context, we can recall some of the happenings in the rest of the world during the 1780s, some devastating, far from the East Prussian city of Königsberg where Kant had his home. In the Caribbean, during the Great Hurricane of 1780 – the deadliest on record – more than 20,000 people perished on islands that included Barbados, Martinique, St Lucia and Puerto Rico. In Japan – a self-isolated country since the 1600s – a famine raged from 1782 to 1787, taking hundreds of thousands of lives, apparently due to local volcanic eruptions. For reasons possibly related to volcanic eruptions in Iceland, approximately one-sixth of the Egyptian population died from starvation in 1783. In Vietnam, civil war broke out between north and south, not unlike the conflict that the country experienced during the later twentieth century. In 1788 the British established Australia as a penal colony with the first fleet of prisoner-filled ships. With a dominating presence in India as well, the British via the East India Company – a corporate entity with its own powerful army – waged war in southern India against the Kingdom of Mysore.

'Cook Told the Maoris that He Had Come to Set a Mark on Their Islands', illustration by J. R. Skelton from H. E. Marshall, *An Empire Story* (1908).

The transatlantic slave trade also reached its height during the 1780s, with over 70,000 enslaved people per year being transported to the Americas from West Africa, mostly on British-owned ships. In Spanish-controlled South America, rebellions for independence began in 1780–83, led by the Peruvian Inca descendant Túpac Amaru II (1738–1781). And, memorably coincident with the publication of Kant's *Critique of Pure Reason* in 1781, the Battle of Yorktown marked the decisive victory of the American Continental Army over the British occupying forces – an army led by yet another of Kant's contemporaries, George Washington (1732–1799).

For most of the eighteenth century, the European nations – France would become the notable exception – and smaller political spheres were governed by aristocratic families, each in command of an army, often intimidating, who passed on their power from generation to generation through other members of the family, generally male heirs. Until the revolution of 1789, the House of

Bourbon ruled France, a branch of which also ruled Spain from the beginning of the century. The House of Stuart ruled Great Britain at the century's outset, but this lasted only until 1714, when the House of Hanover assumed power. The Hanovers were Protestants in allegiance with the British throne, but they were of Germanic origin and controlled a territory in the northwest part of the Holy Roman Empire – a broad association of relatively independent states situated mainly in the area of modern Germany, but also extending into what is now Austria, northern Italy and Czechia. Within the Holy Roman Empire, the Hanovers were beholden to the House of Habsburg, one of the most powerful families in Europe and the seat of the Holy Roman Emperor. The House of Hohenzollern, influential in what is now the northeastern part of Germany, ruled in the areas around Berlin and further east towards Poland, extending as far as the coastal city of Königsberg, where Kant lived.

Given this political landscape, it is no surprise that arranged marriages were common among aristocratic families for both territorial gain and self-protection. The head of one country was sometimes closely related to that of another, precipitating a world where alliances and wars took on a personal flavour. Marie Antoinette, from the Habsburg family – Austrian by birth and married at age fourteen to Louis-Auguste, the French Bourbon heir to the throne – was the queen of France for eighteen years, from 1774 to 1792. Her brother was the Holy Roman Emperor Joseph II, whose relationship to her eventually exacerbated existing tensions between France and Austria and contributed to her execution by guillotine. Philip V, a Bourbon, the king of Spain from 1700 to 1746, was the grandson of the French king Louis XIV and his wife Maria Theresa, who was the daughter of the Spanish king Philip IV. Philip V's hereditary position as also king of France contributed to the War of the Spanish Succession (1701–14) – a war arising from a complex array of competing economic interests in conjunction with a shared fear among the British, Dutch, Prussians and Austrians, who formed a 'Grand Alliance' against Louis XIV, that a single king might rule both France and Spain.

Closer to where Kant was living, the uncle of Frederick the Great (1712–1786), the renowned ruler of Prussia, was King George II of Great Britain, who was born in the Germanic city of Hanover, and who financially assisted his nephew Frederick in his wars against Austria. Sophia Charlotte, the wife of Frederick the Great's grandfather Frederick I of Prussia – she commissioned the Charlottenburg Palace in Berlin which bears her name – was the sister of King George I of Great Britain, George II's grandfather, also from the House of Hanover and born in that same city.

Britain and Germany might have been brutal enemies during the First and Second World Wars, but their royal families have long been intertwined, extending into the twentieth century. It may come as a surprise that Victoria, Princess Royal, the eldest daughter of Prince Albert and Queen Victoria, was the queen of Prussia as the wife of the German emperor Friedrich III. Kaiser Wilhelm, the son of Friedrich and Victoria, was Queen Victoria's grandson. The king of England at the time, George V, was Kaiser Wilhelm's cousin. Another of George V's cousins was Tsar Nicholas of Russia.

Prussia – the kingdom that governed Königsberg during most of Kant's lifetime (aside from when Russia occupied the city from 1757 to 1762 during the Seven Years War) – is often associated with 'Germany' or is understood to be the historical core of present-day Germany. This is true in connection with relatively recent nineteenth-century history, but most of the area that is now modern Germany did not include Prussia, which was an independent state located further eastward in the vicinity of present-day Poland. The area now known as Germany was, for the most part, a patchwork constituted by over three hundred semi-independent states within the Holy Roman Empire – an empire that began with Charlemagne (748–814), the first Holy Roman Emperor – one of which, rather small in relation to the empire as a whole, was the Electorate of Brandenburg, with a history extending back to the 1100s, located in the region around Berlin.

Further east, beyond the borders of the Holy Roman Empire, was the Duchy of Prussia, with its own independent history. In 1618, however, the Duchy of Prussia was inherited by the Hohenzollerns, who controlled Brandenburg, forming the amalgamated political entity 'Brandenburg–Prussia' – a physically separated territory, with the Electorate of Brandenburg remaining within the dominion of the Holy Roman Empire and the Duchy of Prussia located outside of the empire's borders, separated by territory controlled by the Polish–Lithuanian Commonwealth.

This peculiar history, where one part of Brandenburg–Prussia was subject to the Holy Roman Empire and the other part not, accounts for the irregular titles of the rulers of this area immediately preceding and during Kant's 1724–1804 lifetime. Frederick I (1657–1713) of Prussia, cousin to William of Orange, King of England, Ireland and Scotland, referred to himself as the king in Prussia, but he was not the king in Brandenburg, since he was still a subject of the Holy Roman Emperor with the title 'Elector' of Brandenburg. His coronation as king in Prussia took place in Königsberg in 1701, which was then the capital of the Duchy of Prussia and, indeed, not an insignificant city. His son, Frederick William I (1688–1740), also had the title of king in Prussia under the same political inheritance. When he died in 1740, his eldest surviving son, Friedrich II (Frederick the Great), referred to himself similarly as the king in Prussia when he assumed power, but adopted the more impressive title of king 'of' Prussia in 1772, commensurate with his accumulated influence and achievements. His successor, Frederick William II, who ruled relatively briefly from 1786 to 1797 (although not without a threat to Kant, as we shall see) and his successor Frederick William III, who ruled from 1797 until 1840, long after Kant died in 1804, were referred to as kings of Prussia, following the tradition set by Frederick the Great.

Kant, born in 1724, consequently lived under the rule of four different Prussian monarchs, each of whom had his own governing style. These were Frederick William I, the 'soldier-king', who reigned from 1713 to 1740, during Kant's childhood and teenage years; his son Frederick II, most importantly, who reigned from 1740 to 1786 (thus in power for most of Kant's lifetime, ages 16 to 62) Frederick William II, who reigned when Kant was in his sixties and early seventies; and Frederick William III, who was in power for the final seven years of Kant's life.

So far as concerns Prussia's centrality to the history of Germany as we know it, its ascendancy as a European political power became definitive in 1871 when Prussia had grown strong enough to unify its neighbouring states into the area that we recognize as modern Germany. The German Empire was then even more extensive, including the area along the Baltic coastline as far as Königsberg in East Prussia. The well-known Iron Cross insignia – one used in German military decorations in both world wars and still displayed on German military vehicles and aircraft – is an artefact of early Prussian history, for it was the emblem of the Teutonic Knights, the crusaders who conquered the area in the 1200s.

Kant worked at the University of Königsberg, the official name of which was the Albertus-Universität Königsberg, also known as the 'Albertina', named after Albert of Prussia (1490–1568), Grand Master of the Teutonic Knights and, later, Duke of Prussia. The Teutonic Knights originated in Jerusalem in the late 1100s with a group of German merchants who, with increasing power and militancy, were eventually enlisted by the pope to Christianize the pagan tribes closer to home who were living in the Baltic area around Königsberg, among whom were the 'Old' Prussians (a name used to distinguish them from the later population in the Prussian kingdom). The Christianization is known as the Prussian Crusade, which began in 1230 and continued in a vicious struggle for about fifty years, at which point the Teutonic Knights successfully overpowered the tribes and established a Catholic state.

Assisting the Knights with his army at the Holy Roman Emperor's request, King Ottokar II of Bohemia led one of the crusades, after which the Old Prussian settlement of Tvangste, upon which a castle was built, was renamed Königsberg ('King's Mountain') in his honour. Around the castle, three small independent urban centres developed – Altstadt, Löbenicht and Kneiphof – which in 1724, the year of Kant's birth, were united politically to integrate Königsberg into a larger city.

After conquering the Baltic tribes in the 1200s, the Teutonic Knights ruled for the next three centuries until the Protestant Reformation, when in 1525 on the advice of Martin Luther, Albert of Prussia adopted Lutheranism and secularized the territory into one of the first Protestant states. Albert's cousin, Albert of Brandenburg, had been selling indulgences for profit and was involved in a head-to-head conflict with Luther, who publicly objected to the practice in his famous *Ninety-Five Theses* (1517). Later, on the Kneiphof island at the centre of Königsberg, Albert of Prussia established an educational institution in 1544, the Collegium Albertinum, which became the University of Königsberg – a Protestant institution whose origins connect directly to Luther and the Reformation. The Kneiphof island is now called Kant Island. When he eventually became established at the university with a substantial salary, Kant bought a house nearby in the Altstadt near Königsberg Castle, just across one of the bridges from the Kneiphof.

Kant was aware of the Old Prussian tribes' tragic history. One of his students who distinguished himself on his own accord, Johann Gottfried von Herder (1744–1803), wrote a monumental book, *Ideas for the Philosophy of History of Humanity* (1784–91) – one that Kant later reviewed – where he described the Teutonic Knights' conquering of the Old Prussians as regrettably brutal, bloody and unjust. By the time Kant was born in 1724, the tribal population had been absorbed into the Christianized state and the culture and language of the Old Prussians had become extinct.

Many of the world's tribal groups have had the same fate as that of the Old Prussians, among whom are most of the original Native American tribes. In North America, James Fenimore Cooper's

Model of old Königsberg.

Königsberg Cathedral (Kant's tomb is at the rear left corner of the cathedral under the rectangular portico).

novel *The Last of the Mohicans: A Narrative of 1757*, set during the French and Indian War and published in 1826, was written with an awareness of how the French and British were engaged in destructive colonization. When Kant was teaching in Königsberg, his historical situation was not altogether different from those who teach in many of today's universities, where long ago – and not so long ago in some instances – the university land was inhabited by tribal peoples whose presence and cultures have been mostly erased, perhaps remembered only by a handful of surrounding town and street names.

The University of Königsberg, as such, no longer exists. During the Second World War Königsberg was bombed by the British and the city was reduced to rubble. This destruction included cultural treasures stolen from Soviet territories by the Nazis, including over a thousand paintings and icons that had been amassed and displayed in the city. The whereabouts of the staggeringly precious Amber Room located formerly in the Catherine Palace near St Petersburg, the 'eighth wonder of the world', commissioned by Frederick I and originally intended for Charlottenburg Palace in Berlin but later gifted in 1714 to Tsar Peter the Great by Frederick's son Frederick William I, still remains a mystery. Prior to the bombing it had been on display in Königsberg castle.

After the Russians assumed control in 1945 and began rebuilding, the university area became the location of the Kaliningrad State Pedagogical Institute in 1948, carrying the city's new name after Mikhail Kalinin (1875–1946), a Russian revolutionary and politician. In 1967 the institute became the Kaliningrad State University and in Kant's great honour the university was renamed the Immanuel Kant Baltic Federal University in 2005. Not much is left of the Germanic city and culture that endured there for centuries until the 1940s, for Kaliningrad was remodelled almost entirely with Russian-style architecture and repopulated with Russian citizens.

Of what remains of old Königsberg, one visually striking artefact is the Königsberg Cathedral, whose architectural plans date from the fourteenth century. It was beautifully rebuilt and restored during the 1990s and now contains a museum dedicated to Kant and his times. Kant's tomb is connected to the cathedral in parklike surroundings attached to the cathedral's rear. In the nearby university that now bears his name, it gives one pause to consider how the historical experience of the professors who presently teach there is not unlike that of Kant, who centuries ago must have reflected upon how his city and university had been constructed on land that was once the tribal home of the Old Prussians, whose history war and its conquering armies had erased.

2

Pietism, Kant, Königsberg and Casanova

To appreciate Kant's childhood and early life, it is important to consider the religious surroundings in his family and educational environment. These were Lutheran, but more specifically Pietist, in accord with a movement aimed at religious reform that emerged in the later 1600s through the work of Philipp Jakob Spener (1635–1705), a pastor in Frankfurt, and later in Berlin. Adhering closely to Luther's claim that biblical statements supersede dictates that the Church institutes, Spener emphasized the importance of Bible study and discussion in small, intimate groups, the main purpose of which was to intensify and reinforce an attitude of intense faith and piety. The seminal idea is an old one, going back to the Sermon on the Mount: true spirituality resides in the quality of one's awareness, not in external appearances. One's observable behaviour might not display it, but if one privately lusts after a neighbour's spouse, it is spiritually the same as having put those feelings into objectionable action. The purity of one's consciousness should be cultivated, and this is what the Pietists emphasized.

Motivated by Spener's example and more directly connected to Kant's experience was August Hermann Francke (1663–1727), who established Pietist-sponsored schools of the kind that Kant later attended in Königsberg. Francke's personal history and religious perspective are instructive in understanding some of the controversies that Kant, in his own philosophical writings, faced when considering the tensions and possible adjudications between knowledge and faith. As we will later discuss in more detail, Kant's theory of knowledge balanced and combined two philosophical methods: the first was that of Continental rationalist thinkers such as René Descartes (1596–1650), Baruch Spinoza (1632–1677), Gottfried Wilhelm Leibniz (1646–1716) and Christian Wolff (1679–1754) that foundationally emphasized logic, geometry and mathematics; the second was that of British empiricist philosophers such as John Locke (1632–1704), George Berkeley (1685–1753) and David Hume (1711–1776) that emphasized the primacy of observation through the five senses. The two methods respectively embodied a contrast between pure concepts that are innate and raw sensations that are given from without. Kant's theory went beyond this fusion of methods, however, setting limits on it to make room for religious faith, establishing a balance between philosophy as an academically allied discipline and, for example, Pietism as a religious orientation and personal attitude towards the world.

In conjunction with his studies of Hebrew and Greek, Francke's early interest was biblical interpretation, and, like Spener, he conveyed his ideas through small discussion groups, the private nature of which raised suspicions among the established Lutheran authorities. Central to Francke's approach was the notion of being 'reborn' as a faithful Christian through Bible study. Concerning those who remained unborn, his attitude was severe:

> But also the unbelief, in which we are conceived and born, is to be fittingly regarded as the main cause and root of all sins. And thus we are by nature also transgressors of all God's commandments. By nature we are atheists and idolaters. By nature we are all despisers of God's name and his honor and glory. By nature we are all unholy, to whom his Word, like God himself, is a distaste and annoyance. By nature we are all disobedient, murderers, adulterers, thieves, false witnesses, and so on.[1]

Aside from regarding the Lutheran institutions of his time as having failed to instil a sense of faith in their congregations, Francke perceived most people as lacking a genuine awareness of and respect for God's existence. It is easy to profess a belief in God, to give voice

Bernhard Vogel, *August Hermann Francke*, *c*. 1719–37, engraving.

to the words, but living in accord with that belief is another matter. As far as people's lifestyles were concerned, Francke observed that in practice, almost everyone might as well be an atheist, insofar as guiding moral sensibilities and a devout spiritual awareness were mostly absent. In a life-changing episode, he himself underwent a personal transformation from a worldly, secularized consciousness to a more penetrating awareness of God and the meaning of biblical scriptures, and he saw this as an example for everyone. His experience was profound enough to refer to it as a rebirth – one that could lead him and anyone else who experienced the same, so he believed, from a sinful lifestyle to a potentially sinless one.

In his sermons and relationships with his congregation, Francke focused on the intensity of a person's faith and commitment to God and a holy life, judging others in that light. As a baseline condition, he experienced his surrounding world as corrupt,

Sodom-and-Gomorrah-like, and this motivated him to dedicate his life, like a shepherd, to directing individuals away from and out of this profane environment. Programmatically, it entailed the promotion and cultivation in his congregation of a rebirth in each individual from a secular existence into a more pious one, and in this, Francke tended to be uncompromising. He had no toleration for individuals who, despite their institutional power and impressive responsibilities, he perceived as displaying little respect for either the absolute authority of the Bible or religious faith as a necessary condition for attaining truth and salvation.

In 1694 Frederick, Duke of Prussia and Elector of Brandenburg (in 1701 to be crowned Frederick I, King in Prussia, as mentioned), established the University of Halle – an institution that soon became one of the leading lights of higher education in the Germanic world as well as a cultural centre for Pietism. In 1700 Frederick also founded the Royal Prussian Academy of the Sciences along with his wife Sophie Charlotte, and they invited the great philosopher Leibniz to be the president of the academy. Sophie Charlotte, raised in Hanover and fluent in German, French, Italian and English, intellectually and culturally sophisticated beyond her Prussian surroundings, was a good friend of Leibniz and the two had an extensive philosophical correspondence. Leibniz, who had collaborated with Francke in relation to the linguistic, scientific and mathematical aspects of Francke's schools, invited him to be a member of the academy.

Francke was then the pastor in the town of Glaucha and professor of theology and Oriental languages at the University of Halle, a position he obtained through Spener's influence, whose solid relationships with Frederick had been instrumental in founding the university. To spread the Pietistic message, Francke had a visionary conception of education that led him to establish an orphanage, a school for poor students and a school for the children of aristocratic families, all of which developed into a large educational complex eventually serving several thousand students, aimed significantly towards the teaching of languages and the sciences, all with a Pietist inspiration.

Francke's educational complex became a model for Pietist schools within the Prussian realm, one of which was the Collegium Fridericianum in Königsberg, which Kant attended between the ages of eight and sixteen. At the Collegium Kant studied languages – Hebrew, Greek, Latin and French – as well as logic, mathematics, geography and history. Consistent with Francke's influence, Kant's classes in Hebrew and Greek were focused on doing translations from the Bible. His early training in Latin, both speaking and writing, served him well: not only did he develop a lifelong enjoyment of the language, but it was required for his scholarly work at the University of Königsberg, where he wrote in Latin the Inaugural Dissertation for his professorship in 1770, among other works. He also delivered the lecture for his Inaugural Dissertation ceremony in Latin.

Since Kant was exposed to Pietism both at school and home at a young age, it is natural to ask what his attitude towards Pietism actually was. The following is an excerpt where he offered a considered opinion, speaking as a much older man:

> One may say of pietism what one wants, enough! It suffices that the people to whom it was a serious matter were distinguished in a manner deserving of all respect. They possessed the highest good which man can enjoy – that repose, that cheerfulness, that inner peace which is disturbed by no passions. No want or persecution dismayed them; no controversy was able to provoke them to anger or to enmity. In a word, even the mere onlooker was compelled to involuntary admiration. I still remember how once disputes arose between the harness-making and saddler trades regarding their privileges, during which my father suffered much. But, nevertheless, this quarrel was treated by my parents, even in family conversation, with such forbearance and love towards their opponents, and with so much trust in Providence, that the memory of it, although I was then a boy, has never left me.[2]

Kant respected the Pietist outlook as a practical means of developing a solid moral character, given the stellar example of his parents. His mother, Anna Regina, whom he loved dearly, was especially influential. She was a devout Pietist and attended prayer meetings led by Franz Albert Schultz (1692–1763), the local pastor and later professor of theology at the University of Königsberg. Schultz's background was itself impressive: he had studied with Francke at the University of Halle and, even more significantly, with Christian Wolff, a close philosophical associate of Leibniz, who as a professor at Halle taught mathematics, natural science and philosophy. In Königsberg Schultz became a friend of the Kant family and, noticing young Immanuel's abilities, facilitated Kant's enrolment at the Collegium Fridericianum, the Pietist institution of which he was to become the director a year after Kant enrolled.

As Kant mentions above, his family was hardworking in the harness-making trade. With both his father and mother coming from harness-making backgrounds, the family had a financially comfortable position as craftspeople until the business was disrupted by the deaths of Kant's grandfather in 1729 and Kant's mother in 1737, at age forty. Kant, born on 22 April 1724 and baptized as Emanuel Kandt, was thirteen when his mother died from smallpox, after contracting it accidentally while attending to a close friend who was ill.[3] Less than a decade later, while Kant was at the university, his father died in 1746, leading to further hardship for Kant and his five remaining siblings. He was then 22. After a series of infant mortalities in 1717, 1723 and 1729, Kant, who was then the oldest surviving son with the attendant responsibilities, had four sisters and a brother: Regina Dorothea (1719–1746), Maria Elisabeth (1727–1796), Anna Luisa (1730–1774), Katharina Barbara (1731–1807) and Johann Heinrich (1735–1800).

With respect to the influence of Pietism on Kant's early childhood, the situation is mixed. From his caring parents, the influence was thoroughly supportive, as it inspired an overall ethic of respectable character and dedication to hard, honest, work. From his experience in the Pietist school, the rigorous schedule and repetitive religious instruction were the source of unpleasant, if not awful, memories. It is worth noticing, though, that Christian Wolff's influence at the Collegium Fridericianum was more salient than at the other Pietist schools. Schultz, the director when Kant was attending, was one of Wolff's students whom Wolff highly regarded, and in the Collegium, mathematics was taught from one of Wolff's books. Kant used the same book when he taught at the university.

Kant's Pietist-grounded childhood schooling provided an early, constructive exposure to Wolffian thought – a somewhat unexpected aspect of Kant's education in view of the devastating falling out that Francke and the theology faculty at Halle had with Wolff in 1723, accusing him of atheism and precipitating his expulsion from the university under a death threat from the king. Working at a distance from this explosive controversy, Schultz ran the Collegium in Königsberg with a reasonable balance between the Pietistic and Wolffian outlooks that fed constructively into Kant's experience. It should nonetheless be added that unlike Francke's schools in Halle, the Pietist Collegium in Königsberg did not emphasize scientific subjects as highly, an aspect in which Leibniz, in his association with Francke, had an interest and influence.

With regard to the city of Königsberg itself, Kant's home, it is easy to misconstrue its position in the social history of Germany when viewing a map, for its location in the far eastern part of the Germanic territory could suggest that it was nothing more than a backwater, uninformed and remote from the rest of the civilized world. Living in a place of that kind, one might find it difficult to imagine how Kant could have been educated sufficiently to become one of the greatest philosophers in human history. Königsberg, however, was not as isolated as it appears; it was an important seaport along an established trade route that ran along the Baltic Sea stretching from St Petersburg to Denmark. In his lectures on anthropology, Kant described his city with a measure of pride:

> A large city such as Konigsberg on the river Pregel, which is the center of a kingdom, in which the provincial councils of the government are located, which has a university (for cultivation of

> the sciences) and which has also the right location for maritime commerce – a city which, by way of rivers, has the advantages of commerce both with the interior of the country and with neighboring and distant lands of different languages and customs, can well be taken as an appropriate place for broadening one's knowledge of human beings as well as of the world, where this knowledge can be acquired without even traveling.[4]

As early as 1340, Königsberg benefited from being a member of the Hanseatic League, an authoritative organization of German merchants that controlled the trade in Northern Europe, especially along the sea routes. For centuries up until Kant's time, goods had been entering Königsberg from the many ships that docked at its harbours. If one visually considers the architecture along the Pregel River that leads into the main city, the tall warehouses compare closely to those in Gdansk (Danzig) and Hamburg, Hanseatic seaports located respectively on the Baltic Sea and Elbe River that flowed into the North Sea. Among Königsberg's trade relationships, ships would pick up grain in Königsberg and transport them to warehouses in Amsterdam. Stocks for books (covers, endpapers, inside pages) were processed in Königsberg and then sent to book manufacturers further west. Located on the Sambia peninsula – an area that contained some of the primary deposits of amber, a fossilized tree resin – the city was also a crossroads for the amber trade.

With its history on the further reaches of the Prussian kingdom, Königsberg's architecture and atmosphere were significantly medieval in appearance, with its hallmark buildings having been built long before the 1700s. Within Prussia as a whole, its style contrasted sharply with the Sanssouci Palace in Potsdam, near Berlin, which Frederick the Great built for himself in the 1740s in an ornate French Rococo style that was then at the height of fashion, enthusiast for French culture that he was.

Dramatically contrasting with Königsberg – sometimes referred to as the 'Venice of the north' along with Amsterdam, Stockholm and St Petersburg – whose environment had a medieval flavour tempered by Protestant simplicity and conventionality, is the eighteenth-century seaport city of Venice. By the 1700s and no longer the impressive economic power it had been, the city had become the decadent Las Vegas of Europe, a major tourist destination and port of necessary call for those who sought adventure, culture and especially pleasure. It was a key stop on the Grand Tour – the ritual trip through Europe to Italy undertaken by wealthy young men to further their classical education and to experience life in general.

For its visitors, Venice offered a wide variety of luxury items for sale, a rich history of architecture, as exemplified by St Mark's Basilica and the Doge's Palace, as well as gambling and extravagant sexual offerings. It was the home of the great painters Giovanni Canaletto (1697–1768) and Giovanni Tiepolo (1696–1770). The notorious Giacomo Casanova (1725–1798) also grew up there. If we contrast Protestant Königsberg's with Venice's wilder cultural atmosphere, cities with respective populations of approximately 50,000 and 140,000 during Kant's lifetime, one can gain a sense of Königsberg's relatively conservative quality.

To highlight Kant's character as an intellectual committed to reason, it is revealing to set him side by side with two other individuals whose lives closely coincided, George Washington and Giacomo Casanova. These individuals' three lifestyles match up respectively and nicely with Plato's theory of the soul and society – a theory that inspired the respective themes of Kant's three most famous books, his three *Critiques*.

Plato believed that the soul has three fundamental parts or aspects – the *logos*, the aspect governed by reason and logic; the *thymos*, the aspect dominated by emotion and strong passions; and the *eros*, the aspect directed by sensory pleasure. Ideally in a society, *logos* predominates in the rulers, who govern with justice in view of pure reason; *thymos* dominates in the military and police, who passionately defend the state; and *eros* dominates in the ordinary citizens who are motivated by the pursuit of pleasure and are not psychologically well suited to rule or manage social institutions effectively.

Kant fits well among the representatives of reason and the ruling class, Washington with the warriors and Casanova with the pleasure-seekers. The analogy is arbitrary and merely coincidental, but it is also instructive. Each of these individuals was extraordinarily capable in their respective realm, so we are not speaking here about differences in ability, but about basic values and attitude, and how these give a direction to a person's life. It goes without saying that Kant and Washington were accomplished professionals in their respective areas. Casanova, however, was not a mindless libertine. He wrote a twelve-volume autobiography that is one of the richest sources of information about sensuously centred life in the eighteenth century. Kant's collected works are comparably voluminous. The differences reside in the subject-matter and the authors' value systems, rather than in the willpower, intellectual energy and dedication to writing that the production of such *oeuvres* require. As we will see, it was not only Kant's intellectual life that was dominating and profound: the light of reason also guided his daily behaviour.

3

Kant at the University: The Living Body in a Mechanistic World

Kant began his studies at the University of Königsberg in 1740 at the age of sixteen, somewhat early by today's standards. This was coincidentally the year in which Frederick the Great, the new king, having just succeeded his father Frederick William I, reinstated and re-legitimized Christian Wolff as a professor at Halle after he had been banished for seventeen years, thereby rendering his philosophy less of a risk to study and teach. Kant remained in Königsberg for eight years thereafter, leaving the city at age 24 as a mature young man, not only physically, but intellectually. The people he would meet and study with at the university during this time would set his future course, especially with respect to the philosophical issues he would reflect upon in what became a lifelong effort to attain a better understanding of the fundamental aspects of the physical universe and our moral responsibilities within it.

At the forefront of these issues was the question of whether, and if so how, there is a razor-sharp difference between inorganic nature – the stones, clouds, air and water – which appears to operate on purely mechanical principles, and living beings such as trees, insects, squirrels, giraffes and, of course, humans, all of which appear to direct themselves in a more independent way, and, even in the case of plants, almost with a kind of intelligence. Much of what Kant wrote about over the next fifty years can be seen as inspired, developed, elaborated and expanded from the question of what, in very broad terms, amounts to the apparently sharp distinction between the living and the non-living.

When students enter the university, then and now, they decide upon a major field of study. During Kant's time and earlier, the academic faculties were, as a rule, theology, law, medicine and philosophy, which in some universities was called the faculty of arts. As far as the records go, there is no document that records Kant's affiliated faculty, but it is unlikely to have been the faculty of theology, since many years later, in 1792, Kant crossed off this statement on a draft of a biographical manuscript written by one of his students, Ludwig Ernst Borowski (1740–1831), that he was reviewing for accuracy. One of Kant's friends, Christoph Friedrich Heilsberg (1726–1807), also said that Kant was never a theology student.

The professors whose lectures Kant attended were employed in different faculties. Among them was the long-time family friend Franz Albrecht Schultz, professor of theology, who was a former student in Halle of Francke and Wolff and the director of Kant's elementary school. Schultz once asked Kant, Heilsberg and another member of the group, Kant's room-mate Johann Heinrich Wlömer (1728–1797), what their future plans were and Kant answered that he wanted to be a doctor, which suggests that he might have been enrolled in the faculty of medicine. Wlömer said that he wanted to be a scholar of law and Heilsberg said that he wasn't quite sure as yet. As history has shown, although Kant had the intelligence, his mind may have been too philosophically powerful, broad-ranging and reflective to have been satisfied working in the practical worlds of medical doctors and lawyers. He was nonetheless well acquainted with professors in the medical faculty, as shown by his first book's dedication to Johann Christoph Bohl (1703–1785), a professor of anatomy. Kant composed the dedication on his 23rd birthday, dating it 22 April 1747, accentuating its significance.

Kant did not come from a wealthy family, so he needed to find ways to earn money and maintain a free existence while he studied. To secure funds, he effectively did some tutoring and supplemented this by gambling with Heilberg and Wlömer. They played billiards and cards, their favourite game being 'L'hombre', a pastime popular across Europe, also known as simply 'Ombre'. As an indication of its popularity, Alexander Pope (1688–1744) gave this complex, fast-moving, card-bidding game a literary boost in his poem *The Rape* [Theft] *of the Lock* [of Hair] (1717). Kant was an excellent billiards player and his attraction to the game was probably not merely accidental. The image of billiard balls knocking together is none other than a model of how Newton, and of course Kant as well, conceived of the mechanical interactions of objects in the physical world.

The three made good money together and, given the nature of their extracurricular activities, one can wonder what became of Kant's two friends in later life. As it turned out, Heilsberg and Wlömer became successful lawyers with the government, Heilsberg in the Chamber of War and Domains in Königsberg and Wlömer in a series of high-level offices of finance, some of which were in Berlin. Although we can only speculate regarding the faculty in which Kant was enrolled, the fact that his two close friends became respected lawyers is thought-provoking, given how the stylistic tone of Kant's philosophizing attends constantly and consistently to laws, principles, rules and regulations, not from legal books, but of the natural world, morality and the human mind. His manner of thinking had a distinctively legalistic bent, as well as a scientific-mathematical one, although he applied it in the field of philosophy.

The subjects taught in the philosophy faculty might appear to be peculiar at first sight, if not uncharacteristic. In addition to what one would expect – logic, metaphysics and ethics – the professors taught poetry, Eastern languages, Greek, rhetoric, history, mathematics and physics. This is an artefact of how the faculty of philosophy was conceived of as a faculty of arts, significantly lower in prestige and regarded as preparatory to the higher studies of medicine, law and theology.

Among Kant's professors, particularly influential were Johann David Kypke (1692–1758) and Martin Knutzen (1713–1751), both professors of logic and metaphysics, and Johann Gottfried Teske (1704–1772), a professor of physics. We can add Franz Albrecht Schultz, professor of theology and family friend. Their backgrounds were varied, so it is not as if Kant was taught monolithically by a set of adherents to a single philosophical outlook, although there was a consistent Pietistic underpinning. There was more of a mixture of Pietism, Aristotelianism and Wolffian rationalism in various proportions, with the addition of British empiricism. Kypke was influenced by Aristotelian philosophy and Pietism, as was Teske. Schultz was influenced by Wolffianism and Pietism, as was Knutzen. Knutzen was also familiar with Aristotelianism and was reading and translating some of John Locke's works. All of these aspects would be incorporated, albeit transformed, into Kant's great book the *Critique of Pure Reason* (1781/7).

Within this philosophical environment, one of the main issues was the question of how theology and philosophy, faith and reason, scripture and science – all expressions of the same basic conflict – are exactly related to each other. An obvious question, then, is how Kant himself initially formulated and addressed this topic and who among his professors were the most influential in his efforts. Extending back to Descartes, a background worry set the general scene in view of the increasing prestige and predictive power that mathematical and scientific thought was acquiring and displaying. Simply stated, if material nature, that is, physics, operates precisely according to invariable mathematical laws, then everything physical is mechanically determined like a clockwork. If so, then perhaps we are not really free and, more troubling yet, perhaps God is not necessary to include substantially, if at all, in an informed conception of the universe. Science and mathematics were appearing to carry deterministic and atheistic implications.

The threat that mathematics and science posed to theism had been met head-on in a work by Bishop George Berkeley, who in 1734 attacked Newton's and Leibniz's mathematical method of calculus in a work entitled *The Analyst – A Discourse Addressed to an Infidel Mathematician: Wherein It Is Examined Whether the Object, Principles, and Inferences of the Modern Analysis Are More Distinctly Conceived, or More Evidently Deduced, Than Religious Mysteries and Points of Faith*. Berkeley argued that no mathematician is in the position to criticize theologians as irrational, for the method of calculus is itself absurd.

John Smibert, *Bishop George Berkeley*, 1730, oil on canvas.

As Berkeley saw it, the mathematical method advanced by Leibniz and Newton involves adding together sets of infinitesimal points, each of which has no definable extension, to yield results that express a definite extension (for example, as when calculating the area under a curve, adding together an infinite number of parallel lines, each of which has no definable thickness, to yield an area that has a thickness). The procedure amounts to expecting a positive number to result from adding together an infinite number of zeros, or, worse yet, an infinite number of items that defy definition or precise determination, all of which reside in a vague and contradictory area between something and nothing.

Where Kant was living, disputing God's existence was out of the question and Kant himself was a theist throughout his life. Mathematics and science were nonetheless respected disciplines, especially through the influence of Leibniz and Wolff, both of whom were theists, as was Newton. So the question lingered about how properly to reconcile mathematics and God, as well as mathematics and free will, regarded as a distinctively human quality insofar as it was thought that we are made in God's image.

Kant's first book – one that he wrote while still a student – is a dense, almost purely mathematically oriented work in theoretical mechanics, discussing at length the difference in scope and applicability between the formulas mv (from Descartes) and mv^2 (from Leibniz) as a way to measure physical force. Beneath that technical surface, however, it addressed the philosophical question of whether mathematical thinking is powerful enough to explain the free activity that living beings apparently display. If mathematics is not powerful enough, which Kant aimed to show, then there is room to acknowledge the reality of God along with a kind of free activity in bodies for which a mechanical, mathematically grounded, deterministic view of nature remains unable to account.

Kant wrote *Thoughts on the True Estimation of Living Forces* from 1744 to 1746 when he was between the ages of 20 and 22, with a dedication added in 1747. It was eventually published in 1749. This first book, often overlooked in Kant studies, is a striking display of academic ambition and originality for a 22-year-old. From the formulation of problems and writing style, one can see Kant expanding upon the work of Martin Knutzen, marking off his own views and territory in contrast to his professor but, more importantly, distinguishing himself from some of the most respected thinkers of the time. From the very outset, Kant conceived of himself as a player in the intellectual big leagues. In its philosophical aspect, the book attends to a dispute between the Cartesian position – one that acknowledges an interaction between mind and body – and the Leibnizian position that regards mind and body as separate entities, each moving on their own independent, albeit parallel, paths, programmed by God to be coordinated, but not interacting.

Given its unusual philosophical vision of the world, a word should be said about Leibniz's position, which requires a stretch of the imagination. Something also should be said about the relationship between Kant and Knutzen, which may have played into the reception of Kant's book. Regarding the latter, Knutzen was appointed professor of logic and mathematics in Königsberg at the impressively young age of 21. For comparison, consider how Friedrich Nietzsche (1844–1900) was appointed professor of classics in Basel at age 24, which is usually cited as an exceptional achievement for a young scholar. Consider then, the academic career Knutzen might have had, had he not unfortunately died early, only about a month after his 37th birthday. When Kant entered the university at age 16, Knutzen was 26, which is to say that the age difference between them was more like that of a pair of younger and older brothers than that of a son and a father. And as is evident from the age at which Kant wrote his first book, he was as precocious as Knutzen and, we can add, Nietzsche.

Although there are some dissimilarities, the relationship between Kant and Knutzen is worth comparing to that of Nietzsche and Richard Wagner, who was more of a father figure to Nietzsche. Both Kant and Nietzsche initially worked closely with their more famous role models and shared their intellectual interests. During his years as a professor of classics, Nietzsche celebrated Wagner's music as a vehicle for cultural salvation in his first book, *The Birth of Tragedy* (1872). Astronomy was among Knutzen's interests, and he was known for predicting the return of a comet in 1744. Following the same subject, Kant later wrote about the speed of Earth's rotation in 1754 along with Earth's age and published his nebular hypothesis of the origins of the solar system, planets and universe. Given the near-equality of the intellectual abilities of everyone involved, combined with their self-assured personalities, fallings out may have been inevitable as the younger intellects eventually went out on their own. In Kant's case it didn't take him long to do so.

Kant and Knutzen were on good terms at first, with Knutzen lending books to Kant from his personal library. Their personalities, though, were different. Knutzen was more of a recluse and Kant was more outgoing and friendly. Neither Knutzen nor Kant mentioned the other by name in any of their writings, which is peculiar, and it suggests that their relationship eroded, as opposed to their not having had one to begin with. Knutzen died early in 1751, so when Kant returned to the university to complete his master's thesis, he worked with Teske, his physics professor, either out of choice or default. What happened between Kant and Knutzen is a matter of speculation – the consequent silence between the two has always raised questions – but whatever it was, it does not appear to have been socially damaging for Kant. His welcome at the university remained intact and he was later hired as a professor of logic and metaphysics in the position that his teachers Kypke and Knutzen had had, taking over from Kypke's successor.

In reference to Leibniz's view – which was also that of Christian Wolff – it helps to appreciate how the image of the mechanical watch formed a guiding conception of the natural world, if not the universe as a whole, during the 1600s and 1700s. This idea of the world as an immense clockwork conveys the idea of how mathematical predictability can be expected in the workings of whatever natural objects or processes happen to be of interest. It significantly fostered the advance of science.

One way to imagine the watch analogy is to regard the natural world extended endlessly in space and time as a single integrated, immense clockwork. This is the usual way. The universe is a big clock. Another way – Leibniz's, which is inspired by the idea of a dimensionless mathematical point – is to imagine the universe as composed of an infinite number of point-like clocks, each created and programmed by God to run in perfect parallel timing with one another. The sequence of ideas in a person's mind, for example, would be the interior of one of these clocks; the sequence of movements of a person's body would be the interior of another, set in perfect coordination with the sequence of ideas in the person's mind. So when one moves one's hand, it is not as if the action of one's mind causes the hand to move; it is rather that the movement of the mind and the movement of the body are independently matched up with one another, pre-arranged by God. And so on for every other person and every other thing. This God-established and hence 'pre'-established harmony is at the core of Leibniz's metaphysics.

The view sounds fantastic, but it was taken seriously. Not everyone found it believable, though, not only in reference to the postulation of an infinite number of pre-programmed perceiving points, but in connection with Leibniz's associated claim that since God made the world and God is all-knowing, all-powerful and all-good, our world must be the best of all possible worlds. Voltaire (François-Marie Arouet (1694–1778)) mocked this proposition in his novel *Candide* (1759), whose main character suffered continual misfortune to the point of laughability. Voltaire also found it incredible that a drop of urine, of all things, could be composed of an infinity of perceiving, soul-like points. Despite the resistance from such a high-profile thinker – Voltaire was an honoured guest in Frederick the Great's palace – Leibniz remained one of the most respected philosophers of the time.

With regard to the watch analogy as an illustration of Leibniz's metaphysics, and notwithstanding how Leibniz uses it himself to communicate his notion of pre-established harmony, the analogy remains incomplete and misleading insofar as it does not capture the important idea that each tiny clock or 'monad', as Leibniz refers to them, or 'elements', as Wolff calls them, unfolds according to its own given nature, rather like a plant or any other living organism. Each monad has a goal-orientation or teleological aspect and is, God's programming aside, entirely self-determined. As such, the monad acts freely in that it is not influenced or pushed around by anything outside itself.

Since everything is composed of monads – and since each, as a perceiving point, is in a broad sense 'living' – nature is full of life on Leibniz's view. Inspired by this idea of a self-determining, living monad, Kant states generally in *Living Forces* that 'a body possesses living force if it has based the cause of its motion sufficiently and completely on itself.'[1] For understanding Kant, Leibniz's conception of monads and pre-established harmony is essential, for he absorbed this Leibnizian outlook when young, worked with it over the years, detected flaws in it from the very beginning and used it as a jumping-off point for his own philosophizing, often incorporating or transforming Leibnizian or Wolffian ideas into his own view.

Kant's first book is a good example of this, for he adheres instead to Descartes' position, advocating a mind–body interaction, or what was then called 'physical influx', as opposed to Leibniz's and Wolff's

Christoph Bernhard Francke, *Gottfried Leibniz*, *c.* 1695, oil on canvas.

Nicolas de Largillière, *Voltaire*, 1724–5, oil on canvas.

pre-established harmony. The name 'physical influx' expresses the thought of an interpenetration of mind and body that occurs when, for example, one intentionally moves one's hand, or feels pain when fire burns one's finger.

In the same work, Kant argued against an all-permeating mechanistic outlook where every aspect of the natural world could be understood mathematically – a position he would hold for his entire life. One might be able to explain mechanically how a physical body must move according to the laws of nature, but explaining the self-determined, 'living' quality of a body – a quality Kant acknowledged as equally real – he considered to be beyond mathematical understanding, stating that 'mathematics can never offer any proofs in favor of living forces.'[2] Over forty years later, he expressed the same position in his *Critique of the Power of Judgment*: 'it would be absurd for humans even to make such an attempt or to hope that there may yet arise a Newton who could make comprehensible even the generation of a blade of grass according to natural laws that no intention has ordered.'[3]

The two positions that Kant argued for in his first book – mind–body interaction and the denial of mathematical/scientific mechanism as a full explanation for living forces – can be variously appreciated. There is a medical angle and a Pietist angle. Since the book's dedication was to a professor in the medical faculty, one would, at least on the face of things, expect that its contents would connect to questions in medicine. As a matter of personal motivation as well, Kant himself was always personally interested in medicine in relation to self-care, so an investigation that might help decide upon the most plausible medical theory would be of practical importance to him. As noted, Kant also mentioned when talking with Schultz that he wanted to be a medical doctor. In Königsberg itself, although it occurred some years earlier, the city endured a terrible plague in 1709–10 that killed a quarter of its population, so medical concerns were part of the city's collective memory.

From the medical standpoint there was, and still is, a question in medical theory about the extent to which a mechanical (that is, mathematical, chemical) understanding of the body is sufficient to diagnose and treat illness, as well as preserve health. In the late 1600s and early 1700s there were two competing views on this, the mechanistic and the vitalistic. The mechanistic view understood the body as a complicated machine, analysable exclusively in terms of physics and chemistry. The vitalistic view went beyond this by recognizing non-mathematically-describable 'living' forces that also play an essential role. In the latter, for example, one would talk to the patient about his or her anxieties, fears, hatreds and other psychological concerns as a way to understand the person's basic life energies.

Representing these opposing views at the University of Halle were the mechanist Friedrich Hoffmann (1660–1742) and the vitalist Georg Ernst Stahl (1659–1734). Both were outstanding medical practitioners and personal physicians to the king at one time or another. Hoffmann studied with one of the leading figures in medicine at the time, Herman Boerhaave (1668–1738), from whom he adopted a hydraulic (that is, mechanical) understanding of the human body, inspired by Descartes. Johann Christoph Bohl, the professor of medicine to whom Kant dedicated his first book, was also a student of Boerhaave. The use of the hydraulic model in medicine is perhaps most well known from Sigmund Freud (1856–1939), who used it centuries later to describe the workings of our mental processes, also mechanistically.

Stahl's vitalist position recognized a non-mechanical life energy to be an essential, animating component of the body. His approach was holistic, conceiving of the body to be enlivened by a force that manifested itself across the various organs. In this way he explained the goal-orientedness of living bodies and their resistance to decay. Important here is the recognition that the mind influences the body and vice versa: it is a theory of mind–body interaction as opposed to the pre-established harmony view.

Although Stahl's medical theory was not in itself Pietistic, its advocacy of mind–body interaction was nonetheless consistent with Pietistic interests, which associated sin with illness and required a doctrine of free will – one more easily understandable in reference to mind–body interaction than pre-established harmony – to attribute responsibility to people. Indeed, as far as freedom and pre-established harmony were concerned, King Frederick William I, whom the Pietists influenced, banished Christian Wolff from Halle on the grounds that the Leibniz–Wolffian doctrine of pre-established harmony was inconsistent with free will and that its adoption would prevent him from legitimately punishing army deserters, since they could not be held responsible for their actions.

Although Kant's first book used the Leibniz–Wolffian outlook's vocabulary, it argued for positions that were more resonant with Descartes' mind–body interactionism and Pietist religious interests. Kant's advocacy of Cartesian mind–body interaction gave a more pronounced role to the individual will than the competing views, of which there were two: Leibniz's pre-established harmony, with which we are familiar, and the occasionalism advocated by the priest Nicolas Malebranche (1638–1715). According to Malebranche's occasionalism, God sustains all of the happenings in the body and the mind from moment to moment; neither body nor mind acts on each other or upon themselves. For Leibniz, as we have seen, the body and the mind are pre-programmed by God and as they each act upon themselves, they enact their programmes independently and in parallel. For Descartes, in contrast, each person has a free will that can influence how events play out in the world.

Of these three competing views – physical influx, pre-established harmony and occasionalism – the first transfers more responsibility to humans from God's activity. In occasionalism, by contrast, God's activity is all-permeating. In pre-established harmony, it is mostly determinative insofar as God pre-programmes everything at the outset. Leibniz acknowledges freedom, but this is not freedom as it is usually understood, as a person's genuinely being able to do otherwise at any given time; it is a concept of freedom as self-determination, where each monad unfolds on its own subsequent to God's pre-programming, independently of, and hence free from, all other monads. Other philosophies of the time similarly relied extensively upon God's activity, such as Spinoza's pantheism (all is God) and Berkeley's immaterialism, where there is no physical world per se and God places all of the ideas of nature directly into our minds, as if we were spirits in heaven. In sum, without God, most of these philosophies would fall apart.

So in Kant's first book – and he is not unique here, for others also argued in favour of physical influx – we can see the tip of a historical iceberg insofar as the movement of philosophical thought into the nineteenth century slowly reduced God's influence and presence as a mainstay of the leading philosophies, eventually reaching an extreme point in the 'God is dead' thematic that took hold in the nineteenth century. Kant's mature philosophy resides in the middle of this historical road that gradually dissolves God's role as the central playwright of the universe.

When Kant's father Johann Georg died on 24 March 1746, Kant was 21, very soon to turn 22 in April. Among his siblings, his sister Regina Dorothea was older by six years. The others were all younger. Maria Elisabeth was eighteen, Anna Luisa sixteen, Katharina Barbara fourteen and his younger brother Johann Heinrich only eleven. After his father's death, Kant made provisions for his family and settled the domestic affairs, remaining in Königsberg until 1748, when he left the city to work as a tutor.

The reasons why Kant left the university without a degree remain unclear. That he was financially in a difficult situation was a factor, but he did have a successful uncle who helped him out, for example, paying for the publication of *Living Forces*. It has also been suggested that the book's thesis was too controversial to be accepted by the university or that Knutzen stood in his way. Not everyone left the university with a degree, however, and since Kant took steps to publish his book in German rather than Latin – and Latin would have been the language for a master's degree – rendering it more directly available to the public, it is also possible that Kant felt that he did not need to return to the university, or did not see that he would easily return.

Clear from the very start, though, is that Kant was intent on making a name for himself. He might have felt that he did not need a degree and that his ability to think and publish on a par with people such as Descartes and Leibniz would carry him through. This all presents the question of the profession he alternatively would have, or expected to have, in the long run – Descartes was a soldier and afterwards a self-supporting scholar; Leibniz was a diplomat; Spinoza was a lens-grinder – since his university training did not yet qualify him to enter academia or be a doctor, lawyer or theologian.

While working in his first year as a tutor Kant is referred to in church records as a 'student of philosophy', consistent with a longer-term intention to pursue an academic career. But we can wonder whether Kant had grander ideas, given his self-confidence, exceedingly powerful intellect and ambition to be recognized internationally as one of the leading intellectuals of the time. This ambition shines through in Kant's early texts and others perceived it as well. Writing in 1759, Johann Georg Hamann (1730–1788) described with some literary flair how Kant 'would like to be as universal a philosopher and as good a Warden of the Mint as Newton was'.[4]

4

The Theist, Astronomer and Socialite

During the next six years of his life, 1748–54, Kant found work outside of the city as a live-in tutor, or *Hofmeister*, working with children whom he taught at the primary and early teenage levels of schooling. The first three years were spent not far from Königsberg (about 18 km/11 mi.) with the family of pastor D. E. Andersch (or Anders), who lived in Judtschen (today Veselovka, in Russia). Andersch was a Calvinist pastor to the French Huguenot population in the town. French was widely spoken in the community.

The Judtschen baptismal records of 1748 – the same year he left Königsberg – list Kant in October and December as a *Taufzeuge* (baptismal witness). The role is akin to someone who co-signs a will, without the stronger implication of a 'godparent' who agrees to undertake the child's religious instruction in the absence or death of the parents. On the December record, in the same role and ceremony as Kant, Pastor Andersch's son Paul Benjamin, age fourteen, is listed as a *Taufzeuge* along with six others. On the October record, Andersch's wife is listed with Kant as a baptismal witness. Of note on the October record, the entry gives Kant's occupation as a '*studiosus Philosophiae*' or student of philosophy. This tells us at least that when he left the university, Kant felt a closer affinity to the faculty of philosophy and to philosophical studies, broadly considered, than to what was being taught in theology, law or medicine. Today there is a house in Veselovka with a small museum that commemorates Kant's time in the city as a tutor, the 'Kant House', dedicated in 2018.

After Judtschen, Kant moved to Arnsdorf (today Jarnołtowo, in Poland), more distant from Königsberg (about 143 km/88 mi.), which is about as far as he ever travelled from his home city. He lived there with the family of Bernhard Friedrich von Hülsen, where he tutored three of his young sons. As was standard practice for live-in tutors, Kant was responsible for giving the children their schooling and helping around the house. In the affluent families such as those who employed Kant, the tutor was also expected to be a mentor who offered advice and general guidance about living, growing up and future educational possibilities. The tutors often became their students' trusted friends.

In later years, Kant mentioned that he didn't regard himself as an especially good tutor, since he felt that he lacked a special ability to put himself into the mentalities of young children. Soon after he finished tutoring and returned to Königsberg, though, he did consider writing a physics book for children with Johann Georg Hamann. He also appeared to have done an excellent job as a tutor, sustaining good relationships with the families and students thereafter. One of von Hülsen's sons, Georg Friedrich, who was between the ages of seven and eight when Kant tutored him, later entered the University of Königsberg and lived for a time with Kant, who once again served as his tutor. Beyond Kant's tutoring duties – and this was one of the benefits of the position – there was free time to pursue and develop his academic interests.

Similar to how he would work patiently and determinedly during the 'silent decade' prior to the 1781 publication of the *Critique of Pure Reason*, publishing relatively little, Kant used his time as a tutor to prepare his second book – one that he hoped would establish himself internationally as a leading scientific mind. Among others, he studied the ideas of Isaac Newton and the astronomer Thomas Wright (1711–1786) and, inspired by their example, developed a grand theory of the universe's origins beyond what Newton was able to accomplish.

During this period, Kant wrote mainly as a physicist and upon his return to Königsberg in 1754 published two essays, one investigating the question of whether Earth's rotation has undergone any change over time and the other discussing Earth's age. The titles are explicitly worded. The first was 'Examination of the Question whether the Rotation of the Earth on its Axis, by which it Brings About the Alternation of Day and Night, has Undergone any Change Since its Origin, and How One Can be Certain of This', which was set by the Royal Academy of Sciences in Berlin as the prize question for the current year. The title of the second, not quite as lengthy, is 'The Question, Whether the Earth is Ageing, Considered From a Physical Point of View'. Complementing these essays in the following year, Kant published the book he had long been preparing. It had the spectacular title *Universal Natural History and Theory of the Heavens; or, Essay on the Constitution and Mechanical Origin of the Entire Universe, treated in accordance with Newtonian Principles*.

Two general points can be made about these publications, one scientific and the other existential and medical. Kant's early work in physics and astronomy is often underappreciated, if only because the *Critique of Pure Reason* had such a lasting impact. But Kant's insights have proven to be those of an accomplished scientist. In the essay on Earth's rotation, he identified a phenomenon called 'tidal friction' that interferes with the speed of the planet's rotation. Earth spins in one direction while the Moon pulls in the other, creating a friction that cuts into Earth's rotational speed, if in the most unnoticeable manner. In his essay on universal natural history, he hypothesized that everything began with a field of tiny particles, a cloud of dust, which through the simple laws of attraction and repulsion gradually coalesced into the variety of spheres that populate and spin throughout the universe.

Upon such elementary starting points and principles Kant explained the origin of stars, planets, moons and the solar system in a comprehensive cosmogonic vision. He also provided explanations of the formation of the rings of Saturn along with speculations about the structure of life on other planets in proportion to their distance from the Sun.

Kant's theory of the universe's origin, now referred to as the 'nebular hypothesis', is still recognized as a plausible explanation of how stellar and planetary bodies originated. He was aware that he had a fine scientific mind and he saw himself in the same group as physicists such as Newton. His book on the theory of the heavens, he hoped, would publicly establish that fact.

The second point is existential and medical. Kant is not explicit, but his two essays and second book have an existential and medical subtext that concerns life, health, death and finitude. The question of whether Earth's rotation will eventually slow down and stop is about Earth's longevity and eventual death. The question of the age of the Earth is the same, whether it is in infancy, adolescence or old age, which is how Kant speaks about it. The question of the universe's origins has the same resonance insofar as the generation of finite entities itself implies their eventual corruption and demise. Kant might not have expressed it directly, but existential and medical themes reside beneath the surface of these astronomical and cosmogenic investigations, namely, those of life, health and death; not of himself, but of the very Earth upon which we live and depend.

Kant did not submit his essay on the Earth's rotation for an academic prize, but published it in a series of issues in a local newspaper. He did the same with the essay on the Earth's age. His book on the origins of the universe, also written in German and aimed at impressing a wider audience, suffered an unlucky fate: the publisher, Petersen, to whom Kant brought the manuscript, went out of business in the midst of printing the book. A small number of copies were printed anonymously and the rest were confiscated in the business settlement. The book consequently remained unappreciated and relatively unknown, contrary to plan. Its dedication to Frederick the Great, extensive and glowing, if not obsequious as was the style of the time, apparently remained unread by the king. This all happened in March 1755, when Kant was about to turn 31. He was getting older in the midst of these disappointments and needed to think about a career. And he didn't waste any time.

Only a month later in April and again in September, Kant presented academic dissertations to the university, written in

Latin, to obtain his master's and doctorate degrees: 'Concise Outline of Some Reflections on Fire' and 'New Elucidation of the First Principles of Metaphysical Cognition'. The first satisfied the requirements for the master's degree (*Magister*) and was a purely scientific work. The second – a philosophical-theological study – certified him with a doctorate to teach at the university.

Kant's doctoral dissertation was accompanied by a public announcement and ceremony with speeches and a presentation by the candidate, as is usual practice. With an exotic touch, the elaborately printed poster advertising the event was embellished with a calligraphic script in Arabic which read 'in the name of God, most Gracious, most Compassionate' (Bismillahir Rahmanir Raheem). The saying is used to introduce important public ceremonies and scriptural passages, as in the Qur'an.

A month after he was awarded his doctorate, Kant gave his first university lecture on 13 October with the academic status of a 'private lecturer' (*Privatdozent*). As an entry-level instructor, he did not receive a salary but depended upon student contributions, which meant that the more classes he taught and the more students he attracted, the greater were his chances for increasing his income. His employment situation was not unlike that of today's adjunct professors who are hired exploitatively on short-term contracts, are paid by the individual class, are usually provided limited benefits, have limited job security and must often overwork themselves teaching piecemeal at several local institutions simultaneously to pay their bills. Publishing academic works under pressures of this kind to secure a permanent position requires extraordinary brainpower and determination that few people have or can sustain.

Kant was remarkable in this respect, teaching throughout his career for long hours each week, sometimes up to 25, and yet producing influential articles and books at the same time. Still, it is not as if the work never lowered his spirits. After four years of lecturing, he wrote the following to a friend in 1759:

> For my part, I sit daily at the anvil of my lectern and guide the heavy hammer of repetitious lectures, continuously beating out

the same rhythm. Now and then I am stirred up somewhere by a nobler inclination, a desire to extend myself somewhat beyond this narrow sphere; but the blustering voice of Need immediately attacks me and, always truthful in its threats, drives me back to hard work without delay.[1]

Less than three weeks after he started lecturing, a devastating earthquake hit Lisbon, Portugal, on 1 November 1755, All Saints' Day, agitating the minds of people throughout Europe. The widespread social impact stemmed not only in view of the overwhelming destruction, suffering and death that occurred, but in how it occurred, seemingly meaningfully, on the morning of a Christian holy day, when many people were in church, suggesting to some that God was punishing the city for its sins. Most of the churches in the city were destroyed. The event subsequently fuelled publications that either questioned or defended the compatibility of God's existence and natural evil, that is, the side effects of the laws of nature, such as earthquakes, tsunamis, disease, floods, famine, fires and animal suffering. The most well known and sceptical of these is Voltaire's *Candide; or, Optimism* (1759), which, as noted earlier, attacked through literature Leibniz's proposition that this is the best of all possible worlds.

Theologically speaking, Kant's reaction to the Lisbon earthquake was at the other end of the spectrum. It was also of a substantially different kind, namely, scientific. He wrote three essays on earthquakes, published in January, February and April of 1756, that provided a mechanical explanation of the disaster. These essays stand as important contributions to the beginnings of modern seismology in conjunction with the writings of other like-minded scientists such as John Michell (1724–1793) and Johan Drijfhout (1708–1792), who were also motivated to explain earthquakes in purely geological terms. Kant's mechanical account refers to God only briefly, never doubting for a moment that God's existence is compatible with the existence of natural evil. In a 1759 essay entitled 'Optimism', he elaborated this position, defending Leibniz's view that this is the best of all possible worlds.

The earthquake essays and the optimism essay highlight how Kant was immersed in and committed to providing scientific and mathematical explanations of the physical world and its phenomena – this was his overriding interest – and that even in light of a terrifying disaster such as the Lisbon earthquake, his belief in God was unshakeable. Kant might not have been enrolled in the theology faculty when he was at the university, but he always wrote with the theological assumption that God exists.

He was not alone in this. The majority of the philosophers of the period were the same. Descartes is a prime example, who ingratiatingly dedicated his *Meditations on First Philosophy* (1641) to the Faculty of Theology at the Sorbonne in Paris, explaining how he was doing them a public service: he aimed to convince unbelievers who didn't respect the scriptures by presenting proofs of God's existence that have a mathematical certainty beyond doubt. Leibniz, Spinoza, Malebranche, Locke and Berkeley were all theists of different varieties. Assuming God's existence, they explored ways to understand the relationship between God and the world, modifying their conception of God as required. In these thinkers' philosophizing, theology was always in the background.

Kant's theism is especially evident in a 1763 essay entitled 'The Only Possible Argument in Support of a Demonstration of the Existence of God', where he presents an argument for God's existence that extended a line of thought from his 1755 doctoral dissertation. His attitude towards the metaphysical investigation in which he was engaging is nonetheless carefully tempered with an air of uncertainty: he begins the essay by saying that his intention is to provide support, if possible, of an awareness that everyone recognizes: that God exists. For him, the belief in God is a matter of common sense and that if philosophical proofs do not succeed, it would essentially make no difference:

> I do not esteem the use of an endeavour, such as this present one [to prove God's existence], so highly as to suppose that the most important of all our cognitions, there is a God, would waver or be imperilled if it were not supported by deep metaphysical

> investigations. It was not the will of Providence that the insights so necessary to our happiness should depend upon the sophistry of subtle inferences.[2]

He added that metaphysics is itself an uncertain enterprise:

> To achieve this purpose [searching for a demonstration of God's existence], however, one must venture the bottomless abyss of metaphysics. Metaphysics is a dark and shoreless ocean, marked by no beacons. One must proceed as the mariner proceeds on an unnavigated sea: as soon as he makes a landing, he subjects his voyage to scrutiny, with a view to determining whether undetected currents, for example, may not have carried him off course, in spite of all the care, prescribed by the art of navigation, which he has taken.[3]

Kant's reasoning on this matter, which we can mention briefly here, is part of his long-term interest in finding the most plausible support for a belief in God's existence. In 1755 he argued that the world is composed of a set of substances in interaction, and since individual substances cannot change on their own insofar as each is regarded as entirely self-contained, there must be a unifying intelligence that establishes the relationships between the substances and accounts for the changes we see happening between them. This can only be the divine intellect, a kind of prime mover. Without God, there would be no movement at all. In 1763 he took the idea a step further, saying that if God did not exist, then nothing would be possible. Since possibilities exist, then God must exist as their necessary condition. Without God, there would be absolutely nothing at all.

Notwithstanding the plausibility of these arguments, we see Kant's sustained efforts to determine whether we have the power to prove God's existence, and if so, what the strongest proof would be. In his later work, he continued to investigate such proofs, ultimately rejecting the standard metaphysical-logical ones of the kind just mentioned and eventually settling on a moral proof, developing at length what stands as only a passing remark in the first of the above quotes, namely, that God's existence must be postulated as a necessary condition for our happiness.

These thoughts and happenings in Kant's experience were taking place from the mid-1750s to the early 1760s, coinciding with events on the global scene, aspects of which reverberated into the quality and style of life in Königsberg. Tensions began in the French and British colonies in North America; territorial disputes became violent in 1754 and precipitated what is now referred to as the French and Indian War. These two countries' struggle for control over colonized areas – all of which were inhabited by Indigenous people who either took one side or the other or fought independently for their independence – boiled over into European politics in 1756, when Britain declared war on France, with the effect of drawing other countries into the conflict. Thus began the Seven Years War, 1756–63, where – recall the close interrelationships of their respective royal families – an alliance of Britain and Prussia stood against France, Austria and Russia in a conflict. Until the end of 1761, the French, Austrian and Russian alliance had the upper hand. When Russia unexpectedly switched sides, the balance tipped in favour of Britain and Prussia. At the war's end, France consequently lost almost all its territorial claims in North America and Prussia miraculously survived intact.

At the war's outset, the Russian army advanced towards East Prussia in 1757 and entered Königsberg in January 1758, remaining stationed there for the next four years. In charge of Russia at the time was Empress Elizabeth, arch-enemy of Frederick the Great. When she died on 25 December 1761 (on the old-style calendar, Christmas Day), her nephew Peter III, who admired Frederick, took over and immediately made peace with Prussia and returned the conquered lands, although his reign lasted only six months. Owing significantly to Russian internal politics, he was overthrown in a *coup d'état* by his wife, Catherine (the Great). Fortunately for Frederick, the peace between Prussia and Russia prevailed and was solidified by a mutual-protection treaty in April 1764.

During the Russian occupation of Königsberg from 1758 to 1762, life in the city under Russian occupation became more upbeat.

Oaths to the empress were required, as one might expect, and Kant took one with the rest of the university faculty, but the Russians introduced a more open, lively and festive atmosphere, with celebrations for each of the many Russian holidays. Kant attended many parties. Officers from the military, some of whom he befriended, attended his lectures on fortifications and pyrotechnics. During this period, Kant is known for his socializing and for developing connections with some of the most influential people in the city.

As a relatively younger man at the time – in his late thirties – Kant was considering whether he would take up a partner in marriage and his many invitations to parties and social events carried a practical interest. The frequent exposure to a diversity of social groups also gave him an opportunity to observe people. In addition to having the mind of an astronomer, he apparently also had the eye of a social scientist or anthropologist, soaking up like a sponge the structure of the goings-on at these parties and the character types that attended them. The results are evident in his 1764 book *Observations on the Feeling of the Beautiful and Sublime*, published when he was forty years old.

Similar to the fate of his early scientific work that the *Critique of Pure Reason* overshadowed for future readers, his *Observations* is not usually considered at length in scholarly discussions of his aesthetic theory – a theory Kant developed years later in the *Critique of the Power of Judgment* (1790), through which he became known, quite rightly, as the father of modern aesthetics. The *Observations* is manifestly about the aesthetic concepts of the beautiful and sublime, but its discussion of those concepts remains relatively undeveloped, at least as far as refined aesthetic theory is concerned.

There is a way to read *Observations on the Feeling of the Beautiful and Sublime* where it is not mainly about aesthetics, but more about Kant's reflections on the diversity of human characters – a topic more akin to contemporary virtue ethics. He categorizes male and female types, general character types, national types and religious types in view of how they can be associated with either the beautiful or the sublime in various degrees. The four temperaments from ancient medical-psychological theory – sanguine, choleric, melancholic and phlegmatic – for example, are assigned different proportions of the beautiful and the sublime. More generally he associates beauty with female traits and sublimity with male traits.

The book provides extensive and impressive detail, much of which, one can surmise, Kant obtained from observations of social interactions at the parties he attended in the years immediately preceding as well as during his daily meals in local cafés. In this regard, the title of his book, which one is led to assume from the words 'beautiful' and 'sublime' is about aesthetic matters, is better understood if we emphasize the word 'observations' and relate this to Kant's anthropological interests in people. His *Observations* is a revealing work in its discussions of character types – Kant often writes with psychological insight – although it is not a major contribution to aesthetic theory.

The importance of Kant's *Observations* has been minimized by scholars for a further, understandable reason, namely that it contains offensive remarks about certain social, national and religious groups. When seen from another angle, though, it reveals Kant's own attitudes and tells us about the times in which he lived.

Among the remarks that are difficult to identify with – we find these either in the main text or in the notes Kant wrote on the side pages of his copy of the book – are that women's main purpose is to have children, that African, Indian and Chinese religions are utterly benighted, that 'the Negroes of Africa have by nature no feeling that rises above the ridiculous [*Läppische*]', and that 'the Jews, Turks, and Spaniards have arrogance of religion . . . either back-stabbing if they are cowardly or tyrannical if they are powerful.'[4] He adds that since 'all truthfulness presupposes an idea of equality . . . the Jews, who in their opinion have no duty at all towards others, lie and deceive without having any pangs of conscience', and that 'holy bones, holy wood, and all that sort of rubbish, the holy stools of the Great Lama of Tibet not excluded, are grotesque [*Fratzen*].'[5]

Kant's views were shaped not only by his own reflections, but by the times in which he lived, the kind of people that surrounded him in Königsberg and the ignorance that prevailed concerning aspects of common knowledge and decency that we take for granted today. At the same time, there is a side of him that knew better, as he later prescribed in his moral theory an enlightened ideal that we ought to respect each person equally as a human being and never treat people simply as objects to use.

The tension involved here compares to that of the founders of the United States, who in their 1776 declaration of independence from Britain stood solidly on the principle that everyone is created equal and has equal rights, while at the same time many remained slaveholders. Thomas Jefferson, a slaveholder, wrote against the institution of slavery, for example. Both Jefferson and Kant lived in a world that was gradually putting into practice more enlightened attitudes but still remained young, like a flower that had only begun to open.

In view of Kant's socializing, age and numerous acquaintances, the question naturally arises how it is that he never married. One of the women in his life was Maria Charlotta Jacobi (born Schwinck) (1739–1795), an exceptionally beautiful woman by all accounts. We have from her a friendly letter to a 38-year-old Kant written in June 1762 when she was aged 23, inviting him over to her garden, sending him a kiss from her and her girlfriend and expecting that his visit would also get her 'watch wound' ('*dann wird auch meine Uhr aufgezogen werden*'). The phrase's meaning remains vague and some have seen in it a sexual invitation. It could have been merely playful, though, since Maria was already married to one of Kant's friends, Johann Conrad Jacobi (1717–1774), a banker who was professionally associated with Maria's father.

When he was 35, Jacobi married Maria, who was about to turn thirteen, so there was an age-mismatch from the start. After fifteen years of marriage, the two divorced in 1768 when Maria was 29 and Jacobi was 51. A year later Maria married Johann Julius Göschen (1736–1798) after having an adulterous affair with him that became public. Göschen was one of Kant's friends and another of her companions during the early 1760s.

Given that she was close to both Göschen and Kant and ended up marrying one of the two friends, it is possible that Maria also had Kant in mind as a future husband, knowing that her marriage to Jacobi was inevitably going to unravel. Göschen was only three years older than Maria, whereas Kant was fifteen years older, which might have made a difference in her choice. After Maria and Göschen's marriage in 1769, Kant stayed friendly with Maria's ex-husband Johann and did not visit the new couple. There were some apparently hard feelings and complex emotions on Kant's part, since Kant may also have had Maria in mind as a future wife.

The degree to which Kant may have contemplated marriage is tempered by what he wrote to himself about the institution around the same time. The handwritten notes in his copy of the *Observations* have the following:

> This is the age of the rule of women, but with little honor because they degrade the man in his worth. They first make him vain, yielding, and foolish, and after they have deprived him of the dignity of male honor, they have no obstacle. In all marriages, women rule, but also over men of worth.[6]

If we combine this sceptical, not to mention sexist, attitude towards marriage with Kant's position as an unsalaried lecturer at the university, probably unable to support a family, one can say that it is one thing to attend numerous parties and operas and to converse with attractive women where the pleasure ends when the evening concludes. It is a different matter to share intimately a living space with someone, create and sustain a family and commit oneself to domestic responsibilities that could well occupy a good portion of one's time and diminish one's freedom. One must also add to this the Pietist resistance to strong passions implicit in Kant's upbringing, the influence of which is evident in his later approach to moral theory that minimizes the significance of feelings in moral decisions.

Complicating matters as well, the last part of Rousseau's *Emile* – a book that Kant had read enthusiastically – describes at length the characteristics of the ideal wife. After reading Rousseau's idealization, it would not be surprising if he doubted whether good fortune would allow him to meet such a perfect woman, or one with characteristics extremely well suited to his personality. Kant may have thought seriously about marriage during the 1760s, but he obviously thought twice about it.

5

The Best Friend, the Spirit-Seer and the Dogmatic Slumbers

The Seven Years War ended in February 1763 with a victory for Britain and Prussia. On 30 August of the same year, seven men, most of them from England, commemorated their friendship with a tall glass inscribed with their names and a motto written in English: 'Secrecy in love and sincerity in Friendship, all Happy together notwithstanding what happened in the World.' The inscribed names were Emanuel Kant, MA, Anthony Schorn, Joseph Green, Robert Motherby, Joseph P…, John Chappoll and Charles Staniforth. Of the ages that can be determined, Kant was 39, Green 36, Motherby 27 and Chappoll (Chappell) 24, which would make Kant possibly the oldest member of the group.

The spelling of Kant's name is a curiosity, since he used 'Immanuel' at this point, as in the title page of his 1746 book on living forces, rather than his baptismal name 'Emanuel'. We do see 'Emanueli Kant', though, on the public advertisement for his 1755 doctoral presentation. That Kant would use his official name on a glass commemorating a private pledge of fidelity among friends outside of the university is unusual and suggests that given the cluster of English names and the English inscription, the English friends were the ones responsible for the glass, probably commissioning a craftsman to inscribe it, who also happened to have misspelled Chappell's name in the process. The glass stayed in Motherby's family in the generations that followed.

Among the names is Joseph Green (1727–1786), who in 1763 was three years younger than Kant. Reinhold Bernhard Jachmann (1767–1843), one of Kant's early biographers, described Green in

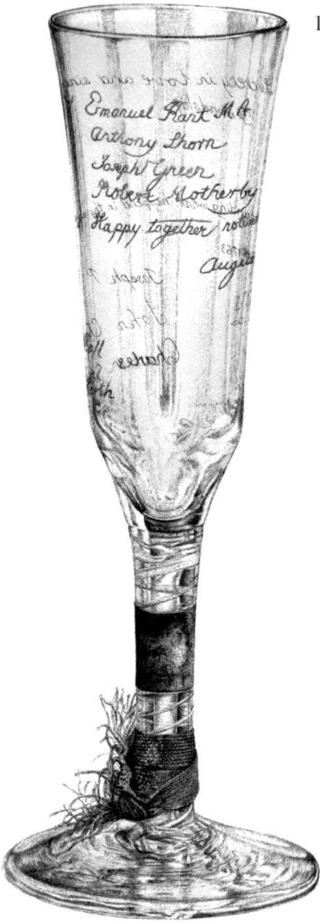

Drawing of the 'Kant Glass'.

retrospect (1804) as 'the most intimate and trusted friend who Kant had in his life'.[1] The two were indeed close, seeing each other on an almost daily basis over the next twenty years until Green died in 1786 at age 59. Kant routinely visited him in the late afternoons for conversation and relaxation before leaving his house at around 7 p.m.

Jachmann describes Kant's initial meeting with Green as having taken place in a park with a group of some other British friends. When Kant commented negatively about the British behaviour in the 'English–North American War' (*Englisch–Nordamerikanischen*

Krieges), not the 'English–American War' as some have assumed), Green became incensed and offended by the criticism of his country. He almost came to blows with Kant, but Kant amazed his friends by remaining calm, explaining his position, earning everyone's respect and gaining an apology at the end.

There is some uncertainty about the topic surrounding the heated encounter with Green, but it must have been controversial and widely known to involve the British government during the French and Indian War – a war that had ended recently, in February 1763, along with the Seven Years War. The date of the champagne glass implies that Kant and Green's initial meeting occurred before August 1763, so the argument pre-dated the American Revolution.

Among the English colonists in North America, serious problems started only after the French and Indian War ended, initiated by the 1765 Stamp Act – a tax instituted by the British to cover some of their massive war debts. Feeling that they were being treated as second-class citizens, groups of English colonists claimed that the Stamp Act was taxation without representation and began to rebel, most agitatingly in the city of Boston. From then onwards, tensions increased until the thirteen colonies agreed to unify, declare their independence from Britain and go to war in the 1770s.

In the dispute with Green, Kant took the side of the 'Americans' – a reference that in the 1760s could have referred broadly to established European settlers of any heritage, to Native Americans or to both. The United States did not yet exist, so the American rebels could not have been the reference. It is a matter of speculation, but the argument between Kant and Green might have been about the expulsion of the Acadians and Native Americans from their homes in the contemporary areas of New Brunswick, Nova Scotia, Prince Edward Island and the state of Maine.

The Acadian Expulsion was an extensive, long-term ethnic cleansing operation mounted by the British during the French and Indian War that resulted in the deaths of over 10,000 residents, mostly French settlers who had developed a culture of their own, but also native people. They were deported to other areas such as Louisiana, originating the Cajun culture there. The British burned towns and farms to the ground and many of the deportees died in transit of starvation and disease or in shipwrecks. The expulsion of the Acadians was sufficiently traumatic to inspire later poetry, such as Longfellow's *Evangeline, A Tale of Acadie* (1847).

So perhaps this episode of colonialist aggression – the ethnic cleansing and deportation of the Acadians – was the source of Kant's objection in the early 1760s to the British government's behaviour and the basis of the argument with Green. The words 'American' (*amerikanisch*) and 'Acadian' (*akadisch*) have a similar sound in German, consistent with this possibility. Also, the dispute was in reference to the 'English–North American War', where 'North American' includes Canada as well as what is now the territorial United States.

Another possibility is that in the dispute Kant was referring exclusively to Native Americans when referring to 'Americans', if

R. Caton Woodville, *Embarking the Young Men*, 1894, engraving.

indeed he did use this term. His lectures on anthropology use the word in this exclusive way. To explain how tense the conversation with Green was, though, we can remember that when Kant was a tutor in the late 1740s with the family of Pastor Andersch, he was immersed in the Huguenot culture – another persecuted group with French origins – whose members lived in the town. When Kant met Robert Motherby, who became a lifelong friend, Motherby was already married to Charlotte Toussaint, who was of Huguenot heritage. They were married in a Huguenot church in 1762.

As averse as he was to colonization, Kant did not highly respect Native Americans as a group, for he located them at the bottom of his imagined racial hierarchy. He recognized four races, the white (European), yellow (Asian), black (African) and red (North American), believing that the white race was the only one with a sufficiently developed capacity for the abstract thought requisite for true moral consciousness. Hence, it had the role of spearheading human social progress. Given this dim view of Native Americans, he might not have been wholeheartedly concerned with defending them. But, sad to say, it would be a different matter with the abuse of the Acadians, who were French and white.

Among the others referred to on the champagne glass were Motherby, Chappell and Staniforth, all of whom were connected to the shipping and trade business between Königsberg and Britain, specifically the city of Hull, where all of their families were located. Chappell and Staniforth, Green's brother-in-law, sailed on ships that exported goods from Königsberg such as yarn from Ermland (Warmia), hemp and flax. Green and Motherby, Green's younger assistant, were connected to Green's father's trading company based in Hull. In later years, Kant invested his money in Green, Motherby & Co. and did comfortably well, remaining friends with Motherby and his family for the next 39 years until Motherby's death in 1801.

From the motto on the champagne glass, 'Secrecy in love and sincerity in Friendship, all Happy together notwithstanding what happened in the World', one might ask about the nature of the relationships between these men. One way to look at it is in terms of solidifying business allegiances, where trust and mutual protection can be central to survival. The English friends were merchants and seafarers from close-knit families whose livelihoods depended upon healthy trade relationships, meeting at a time immediately after the Seven Years War when debts across Europe were astronomical. In August 1763, the month in which the group was affirming their allegiance, banks were collapsing in Hamburg and Amsterdam. Within a couple of years, the financial crisis affected banks in Berlin. So the champagne glass, although it is of interest because Kant's name appears on it, might have represented an effort among the British merchants with whom Kant was associated to solidify their bonds. We are fortunate to have it, for it serves as a benchmark to date the beginnings of Kant, Green and Motherby's friendship.

Three weeks before the champagne-glass get-together, Kant was coincidentally corresponding with a young woman, the 23-year-old Charlotte von Knobloch (1740–1804), about the Swedish visionary Emanuel Swedenborg (1688–1772). She was the same age as Maria Charlotta Jacobi, who wrote to Kant a year earlier with the playful invitation over to her garden, hoping to get her watch wound. Knobloch had written to Kant with some curiosity about Swedenborg's believability – the accounts of his clairvoyance were talked about everywhere – so Kant sent a letter to Swedenborg with some questions. After the letter went unanswered, Kant asked Green to visit Swedenborg on his behalf to find out what happened. Swedenborg replied that his next book would answer all of Kant's questions and apparently left it at that. After Green's return, Kant replied to Knobloch and in passing described Green as a fine English gentleman whom he had met the previous summer, thereby placing the first meeting between the two during the summer of 1762. By the time the champagne-glass gathering took place, they had known each other for about a year.

Similar to Kant and the other well-known thinkers of the time, Swedenborg was impressive in the scope, originality and depth of his thinking. He came from a highly respected family led by his father, Jesper Swedberg (1653–1735), a bishop, religious scholar and chaplain to the king of Sweden. Over the course of his career, Swedberg, who was an inspiration to his son, was also accused of being a Pietist heretic for criticizing the Lutheran church as failing to emphasize the role of faith sufficiently.

Swedenborg first studied philosophy at the University of Uppsala and developed an interest in astronomy thereafter, studying Newton carefully and beginning his career as a scientist with a remarkably creative mind. He wrote influentially about metallurgy, presented ideas for a machine that could fly, studied anatomy and physiology, analysed brain structure and function, formulated the idea of a nerve cell and developed a theory of the cosmos resembling the nebular hypothesis that Kant would later advance. He also discussed Leibniz, Wolff, Locke and Descartes, thought philosophically about the relationship between body and mind and was offered a professorship in mathematics. He was precocious, talented, accomplished and well thought of.

Swedenborg experienced a 'spiritual awakening' that gave him, so it seems, the power of clairvoyance. This was in 1744–5, when he was in his late fifties. With jaw-dropping public displays that appeared to confirm this ability, he became famous in Europe and a favourite among the aristocracy. And his claims were astounding. He said that, appointed by God, he could communicate with the spirits of the dead and could travel in the spirit world beyond the ordinary world of space and time. His writings were voluminous, mostly theological in the later years, and he represented himself as someone whose visions provided him with metaphysical knowledge of ultimate reality.

When Kant first heard the stories about Swedenborg he was impressed, acknowledging that Swedenborg had a special ability of some kind, as we see in his letter to Knobloch. Three years later, and with a dramatic change of heart, he published a book entitled *Dreams of a Spirit-Seer Illustrated by Dreams of Metaphysics* (1766) that attacked Swedenborg with startling hostility. He was not merely critical of Swedenborg but aimed to discredit him entirely. Kant said that Swedenborg's visions were nothing more than daydreams and figments of the imagination, and that his works were completely empty, stuffed with nonsense, and containing not a single drop of reason. Explaining Swedenborg's visions in scientific

Per Krafft the Elder, *Emanuel Swedenborg*, *c*. 1766, oil on canvas.

terms, he said that they were hallucinations, projected images from Swedenborg's mind to a *focus imaginarius* in the way a parabolic mirror projects a holographic image.

Kant's turnaround and the extreme nature of his attack on Swedenborg have been the occasion for speculations about what was going on in Kant's mind. There are a number of possibilities. First, the trajectory of Swedenborg's life and career matched Kant's in its basic contours – coming from a religious family with loosely Pietist associations, developing academic interests in astronomy, natural science and physiology that resulted in impressive discoveries, and then becoming more theological-philosophical in orientation, in Swedenborg's case through visionary experience – except that Swedenborg was successful. He was having the kind of career for which Kant had been hoping. Swedenborg was recognized as a great scientist, welcomed by the aristocracy, known internationally and regarded as an equal to the leading thinkers of the time.

That Swedenborg never answered Kant's letter probably hurt his pride as well. Kant's life at the time had its frustrations. He was not achieving the fame towards which he had been working for years, his love life was uncertain and he was not being awarded the professorships for which he had been applying. He might have envied Swedenborg, not for his views, but for his success as a scientist and public figure. He also might have resented him, outraged by how someone could become so famous and influential through visionary claims that from a scientific standpoint seemed to be nothing more than hallucinations, if not expressions of insanity. If that were not all, he referred to Swedenborg as the worst of enthusiasts – that is, a fanatic – associating him with the aspect of his own Pietist upbringing that he disliked the most.

The literary tone of *Dreams of a Spirit-Seer* brings to mind an early essay by Friedrich Nietzsche – 'David Strauss: The Confessor and the Writer' (1873) – that attacked with comparable animosity the theologian David Strauss (1808–1874). Strauss was famous for denying the divine nature of Jesus, a radically provocative position for the time, which was not too far from Nietzsche's own outlook. Still, Nietzsche criticized him unmercifully as a vulgar philistine, coward and phony with a narrow, dried-up soul, adding the further insult that as a stylist, Strauss was utterly worthless, condemning him in both content and form. In their respective attacks on Swedenborg and Strauss, Kant's and Nietzsche's texts can be seen as verbal assassinations of older, more well-known scholars by younger scholars who perceive them as rivals, if only in their imaginations and private aspirations.

In a letter to Kant from the philosopher Moses Mendelssohn (1729–1786), Mendelssohn mentions that in its critical stance, Kant's tone in *Dreams of a Spirit-Seer* was excessive. Kant agreed and one senses that he was embarrassed. Kant initially published his book anonymously, which itself raises questions given that it attacked Swedenborg so vigorously – one should stand up publicly as an opponent – and the writing is sometimes not as focused as it could be.

To make further sense of the situation, we can add the positive influence that the political theorist and writer Jean-Jacques

Rousseau (1712–1778), whom Kant was then reading, was having on Kant's attitude towards himself and others. As noted, Kant had an ambitious streak and considered himself the equal of the greatest minds of the time. As true as this self-assessment might have been, after reading Rousseau, Kant realized that some humility was in order. He wrote:

> There was a time when I believed this alone [the quest for knowledge] could constitute the honor of humankind, and I despised the rabble who knows nothing. Rousseau has set me right. This blinding prejudice vanishes, I learn to honor human beings, and I would feel by far less useful than the common laborer if I did not believe that this consideration could impart a value to all others in order to establish the rights of humanity.[2]

Kant was captivated and transformed by Rousseau's book *Emile; or, On Education* (1762) – one that in many respects seems almost as if it were written for Kant himself. It spoke directly to Kant's role as an educator interested in assisting humanity. In the style of a *Bildungsroman*, *Emile* describes synoptically the ideal education of a fictional son named Emile from infancy to adulthood, relating in detail the best way to raise a child. But that is not all. After beginning with a celebratory word about motherhood (Kant loved his mother deeply), the book gives during the course of its long narrative examples in physics, mathematics and astronomy (subjects that were among Kant's favourites), affirms that the tradesperson's occupation (which was Kant's father's) is the best kind of work of all, characterizes etiquette for conversations with aristocrats (which was an aspect of Kant's social life), expounds upon the differences between men and women (which Kant later wrote about), offers observations about how to maintain physical health (for which Kant had a lifelong concern), praises Greek and Roman over modern writers (Kant loved the Latin classics), describes the mind's workings in terms of the difference between sensibility and intellect (a distinction Kant later used in his theory of knowledge), maintains that the only true religion is one based on reason (which became

Kant's own view), cautions against the excesses of metaphysical speculation (as would Kant), emphasizes the centrality of freedom in life (as would Kant) and denies that living things can be understood purely mechanically (again, as did Kant).

The degree to which *Emile* resonates with themes and interests from Kant's own life is astounding. It has been said that Kant was so engaged when reading the book that he briefly suspended his daily walks. If true, one can see why. That in later years he kept a portrait of Rousseau in his house says much about how deeply he respected Rousseau's intellect and insights.

Using the Roman emperor Augustus as an example, Rousseau showed how excessive ambition ends pointlessly in despair. Most importantly, with respect to education, he explained that if one is to be a good teacher, it is essential first to be an example of a morally good human being:

> Remember that before daring to undertake the formation of a man, one must have made oneself a man. One must find within oneself the example the pupil ought to take for his own . . . Make yourself respectable to everyone. Begin by making yourself loved so that each will seek to please you. You will not be the child's master if you are not the master of all that surrounds him; and this authority will never be sufficient if it is not founded on esteem for virtue . . . If you do not also open your heart, others' hearts will always remain closed to you. It is your time, your care, your affection, it is you yourself that must be given . . . Be just, humane, and beneficent. Give not only alms; give charity. Works of mercy relieve more ills than does money. Love others and they will love you. Serve them, and they will serve you. Be their brother, and they will be your children.[3]

Let us return to Swedenborg. If Kant felt that Swedenborg's success had taken the wind out of his sails, he also realized that the quest for fame was selfish and that humility was the higher virtue. This tells us something fundamentally good about Kant as a person. *Dreams of a Spirit-Seer* – a book that appears to have been written in

Maurice Quentin de La Tour, *Jean-Jacques Rousseau*, *c.* 1763, pastel on paper.

the midst of some inner turmoil – nonetheless has its regrettable side. The book discredits Swedenborg categorically, a person whom Kant knew to have outstanding intellectual abilities and who deserved more respect. Acknowledging none of this, he published the book anonymously at first and hid his name from the wider public.

Overall, though, the encounter with Swedenborg was momentous, for it was crucial to Kant's philosophical development. Through an examination of Swedenborg's claims to metaphysical knowledge via mystical visions, Kant confirmed to himself the ineffectiveness of metaphysical inquiry in general. Formulating Swedenborg's view in philosophical terms for greater conceptual clarity, he presented a metaphysical 'theory of spirits' that set out the theoretical foundation for Swedenborg's claims. In the process, the difficulty with metaphysical inquiry itself became evident. As we see in the book's title, Kant concluded by associating the 'dreams of a spirit-seer' with the 'dreams of metaphysics', suggesting that in the search to obtain ultimate knowledge, although the conceptual efforts of metaphysics are dubious, the sensory visions of the spirit-seer Swedenborg are worse.

The first section of *Dreams of a Spirit-Seer* – called the 'dogmatic' part – formulates a metaphysical theory of spirits based on Swedenborg's main assumption, that there are two worlds; a spatio-temporal world and a non-sensory spirit world, and that the spirits in the spirit world can influence the course of our lives in the spatio-temporal world. Contrary to Swedenborg's claims to see and communicate with the spirits of the dead, Kant points out that the spirits of the dead are non-sensory, invisible beings. As such, they are in no position to converse with us, since any communications that we receive as humans need to be of a visible, sensory nature. So in the first section, Kant develops the philosophical theory that underlies Swedenborg's visionary claims and, when working through them in detail, draws the conclusion that Swedenborg's view is nonsensical.

Going a step further that could leave a reader dumbfounded, Kant then dismisses his own entire theory of spirits – one that, it is important to realize, he formulated with technical terms taken from his earlier works, writing distinctively in the style he used in the past. He refers to it as a philosopher's dream and figment of his *own* imagination and puts it into company with the theories of Christian Wolff and Christian August Crusius (1715–1775), which he characterized as nothing more than castles in the sky. Like a text that deconstructs itself, the first part of *Dreams of a Spirit-Seer* says about its author, 'This is who I was,' someone who constructs metaphysical theories, and the later part says, 'This is who I now am,' someone who rejects the entire enterprise.

Kant's recourse is to prescribe a more practical, down-to-earth attitude. Rejecting speculative, dogmatic metaphysics, he brings morality to centre stage in conjunction with what he calls practical, as opposed to theoretical, reason. Some realistic advice follows accordingly: since we will never know the mysteries of the spiritual world, the best way to prepare for it is simply to live moral lives. He would remain with this view.

So, beyond the personal hostility towards Swedenborg, *Dreams of a Spirit-Seer* had the effect of sharpening Kant's views on the status of metaphysical inquiry and our place in the world. It precipitated his position that the rationalistic description of ultimate reality – traditional metaphysics – is a fruitless enterprise and an activity for dreamers. An important task nonetheless remains for philosophers: they should attend to the project of determining carefully and precisely the *limits* of human reason, which is a project of self-knowledge. And in this we hear the echo of the ancient Greek maxim 'Know thyself.' This new project of determining the limits of reason can also be appreciated in a quasi-medical sense, or, more simply, as a matter of taking intellectual care of oneself: to avoid danger to one's philosophizing, it is important to be careful not to venture into foreign territory where the terrain is forever obscure and where in principle no map will ever be available.

When writing in 1766, then, Kant associates dogmatism with the style of philosophizing displayed by traditional rationalistic metaphysics and distances himself explicitly from the project. He had his own 'spiritual awakening', so to speak, describing this distancing from traditional metaphysics in the *Prolegomena to Any Future Metaphysics* (1783) as an awakening from his 'dogmatic slumbers'.

In a letter to the philosopher Christian Garve (1742–1798) of 21 September 1798, shortly before Garve's death, Kant characterizes his awakening in terms consistent with the general problem he addressed in his book on Swedenborg. It is that the use of reason to explore the realm beyond experience – the spiritual realm, as described in *Dreams of a Spirit-Seer* – leads to speculations in all directions and yields unreliable results. In reference to Swedenborg, he says that the realm of spirits is a kind of paradise for fantastical visionaries, a country with no frontiers that can be cultivated at one's pleasure. In reference to traditional philosophy, he refers more literally to how basic metaphysical questions – such as whether the world had a beginning, or whether we are free – are forever unanswerable insofar as they admit of proofs that run validly in both directions, contradicting each other and leaving one empty-handed. Such are the 'antinomies of reason' that later form a chapter in his *Critique of Pure Reason*. Kant's references in *Dreams of a Spirit-Seer* to the theories of Wolff and Crusius as castles in the sky are part of the same general idea.

In his *Prolegomena to Any Future Metaphysics*, Kant referred to another, closely associated motivation behind the awakening from his dogmatic slumbers: the influence of David Hume's philosophy. *Dreams of a Spirit-Seer* contains evidence of this as well, for Kant reiterates an argument from Hume's *An Enquiry Concerning Human Understanding* (1748) that he accepted at the time, which was that the formulation of cause-and-effect relationships can only be based on experience and not on pure reasoning. It is not as if the heat on the stove could ever logically 'imply' the consequent boiling of the water. Worse yet, Hume observed that all events seem entirely loose and separate. Ties between events are simply not there to be perceived.

On this Humean basis, it becomes absurd for Swedenborg to speak of causal relationships between the spiritual world and the ordinary world. The entities in the spiritual world are invisible and have no connection to our world. The concept of causality, if it applies at all, cannot extend beyond the sensory world to specify relationships between us and another non-sensory dimension.

Kant's awakening from his dogmatic slumbers was not without feelings of loss on his part, for he admitted that he loved the activity of using reason to speculate about the nature of ultimate reality. The devotion to detail in his theory of spirits in *Dreams of a Spirit-Seer* – a thought-construction he knew he was going to reject – shows his love of sheer intellectual exercise. When rejecting it along with traditional metaphysics as a whole, Kant lost a part of himself in the process – one whose energies he rechannelled into the project of self-knowledge that became his defining philosophical achievement. His interest in science and morality remained as strong as ever, but he now approached these topics with a more reflective understanding of how the mind itself works.

6

The 'Silent Decade': Space and Time as 'Imaginary'

The years 1770 and 1781 are a pair of bookends in Kant's intellectual development, marked at one end by his Inaugural Dissertation as he entered into a full professorship and a steady salary at the University of Königsberg, and at the other by the publication of the *Critique of Pure Reason*, his most famous work. After a decade of labour, the *Critique* brought to fruition ideas that stressed the need for an inquiry into self-knowledge rather than a metaphysics of the beyond – ideas implicit in his 1763 essay on the only proof for God's existence, where he began to express doubts about the reliability of metaphysical speculation.

In *Dreams of a Spirit-Seer* of 1766 Kant's doubts became explicit and they soon crystallized into a clear philosophical vision in his 1770 Inaugural Dissertation with a game-changing, foundational insight about the nature of space and time. As his early biographer Ludwig Ernst Borowski noted about the Spirit-Seer book, 'every attentive reader already found here the seed of what Kant later gave us in the *Critique of Pure Reason*.'[1] Between 1770 and 1781 – called the 'silent decade', since Kant published only a few essays during this period – he expanded, developed and reinforced the ideas in his dissertation, like the opening of an accordion, into a study in the theory of knowledge over fifteen times its length, complicated, technical, innovative and comprehensive, aiming to leave no stone unturned in its 856 pages.

At present-day universities, professors usually teach in lecture halls on campus, sometimes monitored with cameras and recording devices installed in the rooms. At the University of Königsberg, since space was limited to a small number of halls, many of the professors lived near the university and held their classes in their own homes or in spaces that they rented from either other professors or owners of private buildings. Such was Kant's situation for most of his career. The majority of his lectures were held in a series of venues outside of the university. During the 1770s he hired a lecture hall in the same building where he was living – a section of the Löbenicht Rathaus (town hall), which contained rooms for lodgings and lectures as well as a bookshop run by Johann Jakob Kanter (1738–1786), Kant's landlord and one of his publishers at the time. In later years he lectured more comfortably in his own home.

The room above Kanter's bookshop was a convenient place to live, for the shop was a gathering place for academics, one of the attractions of which was the opportunity to see some of the newly published books that arrived in the city. It was a popular locale, not only for its books and coffee-house atmosphere, but for its association with the newspaper that Kanter published – the *Königsbergsche Gelehrte und Politische Zeitungen* (KGPZ, the Königsberg Scholarly and Political Journal) – among whose contributors was Kant himself.

Kant had a knack for keeping himself close to books, as is evident from his residence above the bookshop, where he lived from the late 1760s until 1777. He also worked as the assistant librarian at the Royal Castle in Königsberg from 1766 to 1772 – a competitive position that required an application to the king himself – which was also the university library, unpleasantly unheated as it was. The position gave Kant access to books as well as providing his only reliable salary until 1770, when he was appointed full professor, after which time he soon resigned on account of his increased duties and his new source of income, almost three times what he was making at the library.

One might assume that as a professor of logic and metaphysics, Kant's lectures focused exclusively on these topics and indeed they did to a great extent. He lectured on logic and metaphysics for 41 years in sequence, almost every year that he taught, from 1755 to 1796. With a comparable frequency he also lectured on physical geography – an account of the oceans, rivers, lands, earthquakes, winds, plants, animals and notable features of the different continents – in an effort to provide his students with a realistic, practical understanding of the natural environment in which people live.

Complementing his lectures on physical geography, Kant lectured on 'anthropology', beginning in 1772 with a similar motivation, teaching this subject every year until he retired. For him, anthropology concerned the nature of the human being broadly considered, which included an account of our basic psychological features in conjunction with the social aspects of the differences between the sexes and national characters, some of the materials for which he imported from his earlier *Observations on the Feeling of the Beautiful and Sublime*. From the 1750s to the 1790s he also lectured on moral philosophy, although with a lesser frequency. Other courses in various years included natural law, physics, pedagogy, mathematics, theology, introduction to philosophy and Latin.

By all accounts, Kant was an inspiring, dedicated teacher, interested not merely in conveying information but in motivating his students to think for themselves. Aiming his lectures at the average student, not worrying about the extremely talented who could work on their own or those who were unable to understand him at all, he taught not only philosophy but how to philosophize, working hard on his lectures, filling them with entertaining anecdotes and references and drawing relatively large audiences that included not only students but other colleagues and people from the community.

As someone who began as a private lecturer whose income depended entirely upon student enrolments, his meaningful and captivating dedication to teaching is not surprising. The following is an entertaining example from Kant's 1775–6 lectures on anthropology – an example he included in his lectures for the next twenty years – one of his most highly attended and popular courses:

> Thus someone does state about Heidegger [John James Heidegger (1666–1749), a Swiss music impresario] that he had

> such a bad facial proportion, that one could not look at him without laughing; likewise he also made jokes about it himself, since he once said he was the ugliest person in the social gathering. When a bet was then made, the other person who had made the bet with him, led an old woman in. All now began to laugh still more about her, as a result of which he lost his bet; however he said: it was still not yet settled with this, because the judgment was here passed from two points of view, and one should put his wig on the woman and her cap on him. As soon as this was done, one realized that he was correct.[2]

Kant had a keen interest in anthropology, for he regarded it as a study essential to the practical reality of trying to live a moral life. He believed that it is important not simply to listen to the sayings and prescriptions that one might hear from a preacher or pastor, but to understand objectively and specifically the features of the human being that both assist and hinder the implementation of moral precepts in daily life. In order to live a moral life, knowing one's natural constitution as a human being is of crucial assistance. Indeed, the subject of anthropology was so important to Kant that we have a 1768 portrait of him from a few years before he began lecturing on anthropology – one that his landlord Kanter commissioned for display in the bookshop – that shows him holding a book entitled *Anthropologie oder Naturkenntnis des Menschen* (Anthropology or the Natural Science of the Human Being). Kant regarded himself as an innovator in this subject and hoped that with its presentation he could advance to a less superficial, more sophisticated intellectual level, the moral sayings that one might hear in a church sermon into a more workable and pragmatic intellectual context, the overall purpose of which would be to foster the moral progress of society in general.

In connection with this effort was Kant's enthusiastic support for an extremely progressive school for its time, the Philanthropinum, located in Dessau and started by Johann Bernhard Basedow (1724–1790), who was inspired by Enlightenment values and the educational views of Locke and Rousseau. With a varied curriculum

Johann Gottlieb Becker, *Immanuel Kant*, 1775, oil on canvas.

that included languages, science, outdoor classes, physical exercise and sports such as fencing and gymnastics, the school aimed to promote the all-round development of character in its students, aiming to instil a lasting sense of dedication to the welfare of others.

Kant did much to assist the Philanthropinum. He recommended that the institution accept the son of his good friend Robert Motherby, wrote supportive articles about it in his landlord

Kanter's political newspaper and highlighted it in his anthropology lectures from 1775 to 1776, where he said the following:

> The present Basedowian institutes are the first that have come about according to the perfect plan of education. This is the greatest phenomenon which has appeared in this century for the improvement of the perfection of humanity, through it all schools in the world will receive another form, and the human race will thereby be freed from the constraints of the prevailing schools.[3]

Kant's lecturing at the university consequently had a self-consciously formulated double aspect: a theoretical component that emphasized metaphysics, the theory of knowledge and moral theory; and a pragmatic component that emphasized physical geography and anthropology. His Inaugural Dissertation of 1770 crucially developed the theoretical component with, as noted, an innovative account of the nature of space and time based on a crucial distinction between the 'sensible' and the 'intelligible', which we can now consider.

Central to Kant's Inaugural Dissertation and the theory of knowledge that later emerges from it in the *Critique of Pure Reason* is a distinction between 'perception' and 'conception', or, as Kant expresses it, between the 'sensible' and the 'intelligible'. Descartes expressed the distinction many years earlier in his *Meditations on First Philosophy* by showing the difference between 'imagination' and 'pure intellection': if, as he described it in the Sixth Meditation, we form a mental image of a regular 1,000-sided figure – a chiliagon – and try to contrast this with a mental image of some other many-sided figure, say, a 999-sided figure, the two mental images will be indistinguishable. But since we effortlessly conceptualize the distinction between a 1,000-sided figure and a 999-sided figure, it becomes clear that different parts of the mind are at work in the two cases. One part of the mind deals with mental images, perceptions and sensations, and the other with concepts and pure thoughts.

Kant accordingly drew a distinction between our sensibility-related and our purely intellectual capacities, locating them in different 'faculties' of the mind. Although Descartes had already appreciated the difference between imagination and intellection, within Kant's intellectual environment this ran contrary to what had become a standardly accepted Leibnizian position that perceptions are nothing more than confused conceptions, where perceptions and conceptions reside on a continuum. Kant made it a point to argue otherwise:

> From this one can see that the sensitive is poorly defined as that which is more confusedly cognised, and that which belongs to the understanding as that of which there is a distinct cognition. For these are only logical distinctions which do not touch at all the things given, which underlie every logical comparison. Thus, sensitive representations can be very distinct and representations which belong to the understanding can be extremely confused.[4]

Kant relied upon the distinction between 'sensibility' and 'understanding' at the foundation of his mature theory of knowledge. To commence this theory in his Inaugural Dissertation, he presented an account of space and time that located them squarely in the part of the mind which concerns our openness to sensations, or 'sensibility', understanding them as the *forms* of sensibility knowable a priori that we bring to experience.

To appreciate Kant's thoughts on space and time, consider the idea that space is 'an infinite sphere whose centre is everywhere' – an idea whose history reaches back to Nicholas of Cusa (1401–1464), philosopher, mathematician, jurist and cardinal, and Blaise Pascal (1623–1662), mathematician, scientist and philosopher, two thinkers who associated the idea with God and nature respectively. So paradoxical, it stretches the imagination even when we describe the infinite sphere in a limited way exclusively in reference to space. Standing here right now, we feel as if we are at the centre of an infinite sphere extending in all directions endlessly, up, down, sideways and below, filled with virtually uncountable stars and galaxies. If we were in a spaceship 100 million miles away from Earth, our perception of space would be the same: it would be experienced as an infinite sphere where we felt ourselves to be at the exact centre. And so it would be for any place we might find ourselves in the universe, however far or near from our present location. The format is the same, almost as if we were carrying it around with us.

Now imagine that one is in a canoe paddling down a river. As usual, the coastline is understood to move past, as we assume naturally that the coastline is standing still, and that the coastline's perceived movement is none other than the canoe's own. For centuries, strangely enough, but also understandably, since we do not feel Earth moving beneath us as it rotates, this kind of observation was never applied to our perception of the movements of the celestial bodies. The fact is, though, that just as the canoe rows past the coastline and the coastline appears to move, the rotating Earth spins past the stars, Sun and Moon above and those objects appear to move, as if we were spinning on a carousel watching the people standing on the ground. As with the paddling canoe and moving coastline, the perceived movement of the celestial bodies is none other than our own movement. Such is the astronomical insight behind the historical shift from the geocentric assumption – that Earth stands still in the solar system and the planets and Sun move around it – to the revolutionary heliocentric assumption that the Sun stands still while the planets circle in orbit: the Copernican revolution in astronomy.

Kant later characterized his theory of knowledge as inspired by this Copernican idea, since he argued far more generally, extensively and radically that the ordinary appearances of objects – not only the celestial bodies, but *all* objects such as tables, chairs, trees, mountains and the rest of nature – are not showing these objects to us as they are in themselves independently. The ordinary appearances of objects are rather an artefact, reflection and construction from patterns that our own minds project. There is a sense in which 'we' create the world experienced in space and time. Its distinctive appearance arises from its own mental activity, which is to say that when one looks out at the world, there is a sense in which one is looking into a mirror and seeing one's own reflection.

Such is Kant's foundational claim in his Inaugural Dissertation about the nature of space and time, which he maintains are not realities independent of us, but – a claim perhaps mind-boggling to hear at first and difficult to accept, as counterintuitive as it is – are structures of our own minds that we carry around with us as interpretive vehicles for the reality that is independently there. One could say loosely that on Kant's view, space and time compare functionally to the prismatic structure of a fly's eye that gives structure to the fly's experience as being prismatic, necessarily and unavoidably for the fly, even though the reality within which it lives is not itself prismatically structured.

And so it is analogously for us with regard to the forms of space and time. Kant goes so far as to refer to them as 'imaginary' insofar he maintains that to the best of our knowledge, they have no independent reality apart from us. Whatever ultimate reality happens to be – some speculate that it is God – it is a reality neither spatial nor temporal, but when it touches us, which of course it does constantly, we experience it, along with ourselves, as situated within a spatial and temporal expanse. So just as the celestial bodies appear to move because it is we ourselves who are moving, the world as a whole appears to be situated in space and time because it is we who are using a spatio-temporal format to apprehend whatever that mind-independent, non-spatial and non-temporal ultimate reality happens to be. We open our eyes in the morning and extending before us each day is a spatio-temporal theatre, the appearance of which – in its three-dimensionality and movement in time – arises from the activity of our own minds. We create that appearance.

Hence arises a philosophical problem that troubled philosophers in the wake of Kant's *Critique of Pure Reason*, for the inevitable implication is that whatever the mind-independent, non-spatial and non-temporal ultimate reality happens to be, it is unknowable as it is in itself. Its true nature must remain a mystery, for we can apprehend only how it appears in our human, spatio-temporal way, just as a fly can apprehend the world only prismatically.

It is fascinating that the basic insight underlying Kant's revolutionary account of space and time is not foreign to the human imagination, for we see it expressed at an earlier time in a different context and culture by a major figure in the history of Buddhist thought, Huineng (638–713 CE), the sixth patriarch of the Chan (Zen) school of Buddhism:

> One day Hui Neng thought, 'The time has come to spread the Dharma. I cannot stay in hiding forever.' Accordingly, he went to Fa Hsing Monastery in Kuang Chou where Dharma Master Yin Tsung was giving lectures on The Nirvana Sutra. At that time there were two bhikshus [monks] who were discussing the topic of the wind and a flag. One said, 'The wind is moving.' The other said, 'The flag is moving.' They argued incessantly. Hui Neng stepped forward and said, 'The wind is not moving, nor is the flag. Your minds, Kind Sirs, are moving.' Everyone was startled.[5]

Although there is relatively less information on Kant's activities between 1770 and 1781 – he had a heavy teaching schedule and was working hard on the *Critique of Pure Reason* – informative here is his correspondence with a variety of people that included Marcus Herz (1747–1803), who had been one of Kant's favourite students; Johann Heinrich Lambert (1728–1777), mathematician and scientist; Johann Georg Sulzer (1720–1779), mathematician and aesthetician; Johann Caspar Lavater (1741–1801), poet, physiognomist and theologian; Christian Heinrich Wolke (1741–1825) and Johann Bernhard Basedow (1724–1790), educators; and Moses Mendelssohn, philosopher. The correspondence reveals much about Kant's personal character and the development of the *Critique of Pure Reason*, especially his letters to Herz.

Originally anticipating the development of his Inaugural Dissertation into a single book with three parts, on knowledge, morality and aesthetics, the section on knowledge and truth – published later as the *Critique of Pure Reason* – became so lengthy and complicated in an effort to develop a solidly argued position that it became a book of its own, the so-called 'first' *Critique*. Some years after its 1781 publication and after a second, revised edition in 1787, Kant completed the studies on morality and aesthetics for

Johann Friedrich Weitsch, *Marcus Herz*, 1795, oil on canvas, detail.

Anton Graff, *Moses Mendelssohn*, 1771, oil on canvas.

the 'second' (1788) and 'third' (1790) *Critiques*, entitled respectively the *Critique of Practical Reason* (on the will and goodness) and the *Critique of the Power of Judgment* (on feelings, the beautiful, the sublime and goal-oriented entities such as living organisms). These three books loosely follow the pattern of Plato's tripartite theory of the soul, as mentioned earlier, which emphasized abstract concepts, willpower and feeling as coordinated with the concepts of truth, goodness and beauty respectively. Kant's three *Critiques* are technical and densely argued, but their inspirational core resonates directly with the ancient Greek philosophical tradition.

Kant's correspondence also reveals an unexpected motivation for his theory, also traditionally inspired: less by the Greeks than by the first book of the Hebrew scriptures at Genesis 1:27 that characterizes human beings as having been made in God's image. Consider, then, God's act of creating the universe through an act of pure thought or 'intellectual intuition', as Kant refers to it. Humans lack this divine capacity, but if we are made in God's image, we can expect to discover in ourselves a comparable capacity in a weaker, finite form. And this is what Kant articulates philosophically in his theory of knowledge. If the forms of space and time are merely aspects of our own mind, then, as noted, when we come into contact with whatever ultimate reality happens to be, we create that infinitely expansive theatre that spreads out before us when we open our eyes each morning. We might not have the capacity to create a world out of nothing, but if stimulated by something 'given' to us from without, we can exercise our creative capabilities, automatically shaping that 'given' according to the forms of space and time and thereby creating a world for ourselves. Although one might not expect this, Kant's theory of knowledge can accordingly be seen as an expression of how humans are made in God's image, albeit in a distinctively finite form appropriate to the limited kind of beings that we are.

Related to this, Kant's correspondence reveals how he conceives of morality as a discipline that provides us with absolute directives – insofar as they are absolute, they can be called 'divine' – that define our duties as rational beings. Kant had limited patience for ordinary religious practices with their attendant ceremonies and rituals, for he regarded these as merely contingent vehicles to express the true core of all religions, that is, their universal moral content – a content that directs us unconditionally to respect other people, not use them as mere tools. He anticipated the day when the ceremonies, rituals and localized dogmatic beliefs of traditional religions, along with their superficial differences, would fade away altogether, all demythologized, leaving in their place only a pure moral awareness guided by rationality – a single, true, universalistic moral religion of humanity as a whole.

These ideas are in Kant's letters to the theologian Johann Caspar Lavater and Marcus Herz, his former student and later good friend. Herz served at Kant's Inaugural Dissertation ceremony with honour as the appointed 'respondent' (that is, advocate) – the person whose role is publicly to defend the dissertation in the face of opposing questions. After his studies with Kant, Herz became a highly respected medical doctor and professor in Berlin, lecturing on Kant's philosophy.

In a letter from August 1777, Kant praised Herz as 'that rare student who makes all the effort that goes into my often thankless job seem amply rewarded', adding that their friendship was 'all the more delightful because it springs from the pure sources of an excellent understanding'.[6] Their relationship was trusting enough for Kant to ask for medical advice to remedy the digestive ailments he was experiencing:

> Of the various indispositions that constantly plague me and often make me interrupt my intellectual endeavors (heartburn seems to be the general cause, though I seem to all my acquaintances just as healthy as I was twenty years ago), there is one complaint you may be able to help me with: I am not exactly constipated, but I have such a difficult and usually insufficient evacuation every morning that the remaining feces that accumulate become the cause, as far as I can tell, not only of that gas I mentioned but also of my clouded brain . . . He [Kant's doctor] says that the strongest of diuretics is jalap resin [resinam Jalappae] and that senna leaves and rhubarb are milder, though both of them are classified as hydragogic purgatives. On the other hand, he regards crystals of cream of tartar and tamarinds as eccoprotic, which is what I need. Herr Mendelssohn says that he himself has found the latter useful and that it consists of the pulp of the tamarinds. I would be most grateful to you if you would write me a prescription for this, which I could use from time to time.[7]

Kant also evidently discussed his health problems with Moses Mendelssohn during the latter's visit to Königsberg – the two had been corresponding for the previous ten years but only met personally in 1777, just before the above letter to Herz. Both slight of frame and physically misshapen – Kant's shoulders were uneven and Mendelssohn was hunchbacked – they probably felt an immediate affinity upon seeing each other. Kant trusted Mendelssohn with personally intimate matters. Mendelssohn was not a medical doctor like Herz, but a fellow philosopher and friend for whom Kant had tremendous respect:

> Today Herr Mendelssohn, your worthy friend and mine (for so I flatter myself), is departing. To have a man like him in

> Königsberg on a permanent basis, as an intimate acquaintance, a man of such gentle temperament, good spirits, and enlightenment – how that would give my soul the nourishment it has lacked so completely here, a nourishment I miss more and more as I grow older![8]

Herz and Mendelssohn were both Jews, and Kant had an unprejudiced attitude towards the Jews with whom he socialized. He recommended that Isaac Abraham Euchel, a Jewish student, be appointed professor of oriental studies when he was dean of the philosophy faculty in 1786. The memory of Kant's open-minded attitude endured for decades after his death, as we can see from how the German novelist and women's rights activist Fanny Lewald (1811–1889) recalled Kant's greetings to her grandfather on his daily walk in her autobiography:

> People treated the grandfather with special respect and how even Professor Kant always greeted him with friendliness on his daily summer walks when he saw him at his usual place at the window or sitting on the bench in front of the door. At that time in Königsberg it was still a matter of honour for a Jew to be treated with respect by a Christian.[9]

Mendelssohn's visit to Königsberg had a dual purpose. One was to confer with Kant about a request to him by Karl Abraham Freiherr von Zedlitz (1731–1793) – the person to whom Kant would dedicate the *Critique of Pure Reason* and Prussian minister of justice and minister of culture and education – to find a suitable replacement for a recently deceased professor at the University of Halle (Zedlitz later offered Kant the position, but Kant declined). The second was to settle a dispute between the local Jewish community and the synagogue inspector Georg David Kypke (1724–1779), professor of oriental languages at the University of Königsberg and a long-time acquaintance of Kant.

A word should be said about Zedlitz, who was a forward-thinking administrator who had great respect for Kant. Unlike many contemporary university administrators who drain financial support from the liberal arts in favour of funding more 'practical' subjects, Zedlitz appreciated the value in a humanities-inclusive education and tried to enlist Kant to teach at a more prestigious university:

> Give me the means of keeping university students away from the 'bread and butter' subjects and making it clear to them that the little bit of jurisprudence, and even theology and medicine, will be infinitely easier and its application far more for sure for the students with a greater knowledge of philosophy, and that they will only be judges, lawyers, preachers or doctors for a few hours each day, while for so many hours they will be men, for which they will need quite different forms of knowledge; I want you to teach me how to make all of this clear to the students.[10]

Kant knew Kypke from childhood. They were born in the same year, attended the Collegium Fridericianum in their early education and later became university colleagues. Kypke's uncle was one of Kant's professors when he was at the university and Kant lived with either the uncle or with Kypke when he started out as a private lecturer, using that family's lecture hall for his first lecture at the university. Given this history, it is likely that Mendelssohn asked Kant about Kypke's character to help him in dealing with the conflict between Kypke and the Jewish community.

Kypke, as a professor of oriental languages at the University of Königsberg, knew the Hebrew language; his supplementary post of synagogue inspector for Königsberg gave him the responsibility of attending all services to ensure that the law was being followed. He did this for over twenty years, from 1755. A problem with the Jewish community emerged concerning Kypke's accusation of violations of a 1703 law that prohibited the recitation of some key lines in a central Jewish prayer – lines that were perceived to denigrate Jesus and Christians in general, which was not allowed. Often recited during religious services, the lines specifically condemned idolators – worshippers of a false god – where at the vocalization of the words, the people reciting the prayer would spit on the ground. Mendelssohn explained in his supportive letter for the congregation that since the prayer pre-dated Jesus and Christianity, it was impossible for either Jesus or Christians to be the intended reference and meaning of the passage. The government accepted this interpretation.

From a more matter-of-fact standpoint, it stands that since Christians believe that Jesus is the son of God – a fact that the Jewish community as well as Mendelssohn were aware – Jesus would be perceived as a false god and his worshippers would be included as idolators in the passage's condemnation. That reality notwithstanding, Mendelssohn's mission was to protect the Jewish community from further harassment and in this he was successful. Kypke's position was soon dissolved to end seventy years of external monitoring of religious services.

From what has been said so far, Kant's relationship to members of the Jewish community (as well as others) appears to have been unprejudiced, open-minded and based exclusively on the quality of a person's character. This may have been so in his dealings with individuals on a one-to-one basis, but it remains that he did not sympathize with Jewish religious beliefs. He was unsympathetic with the specific dogmas of any religion, but he objected to Judaism, Islam and Hinduism on the grounds that in his view, each operates with dual ethics: one set of ethical standards for the adherents of the religion that prescribes mutual respect between members of the in-group, and another for whom manifestly unethical behaviour is allowed. In *The Conflict of the Faculties*, he states this explicitly: 'The Jews, Mohammedans, and Hindus, however, refuse to recognize as a law anything that differs from theirs, and give other peoples, who do not have exactly the same ecclesiastical rites as theirs, the title of reprobation (Goj, Dschaur, etc.) – that is, of infidels.'[11]

An extreme version of this in-group versus out-group mentality is exemplified by the 'master morality' that Friedrich Nietzsche describes in his *Beyond Good and Evil* (1886):

> A morality of the ruling group, however, is most alien and embarrassing to the present taste in the severity of its principle

> that one has duties only to one's peers; that against beings of a lower rank, against everything alien, one may behave as one pleases or 'as the heart desires,' and in any case 'beyond good and evil' – here pity and like feelings may find their place.[12]

Diametrically opposed to this Nietzschean vision, inspired by a respect for the rationality inherent in every person, Kant formulated a universal ethics based on reason that transcends the differences between people, placing everyone on a level moral playing field. Close to the spirit of the French revolutionaries, he anticipated a gradual dissolution of conventional religious differences and the unification of society as humanity advanced in overall moral awareness: 'But this division of sects, too, must disappear in time, leading, at least in spirit, to what we call the conclusion of the great drama of religious change on earth (the restoration of all things), when there will be only one shepherd and one flock.'[13]

Some have taken Kant's unsympathetic remarks about Judaism and have referred to him indiscriminately as an antisemite. His relationships with Herz and Mendelssohn, along with his other Jewish students and friends, as well as his general behaviour towards others, suggest otherwise. It is not inconsistent to disagree with a person's belief system and yet treat them with respect as a human being, although admittedly, there can be a measure of psychological conflict in such relationships.

Consider, though, the case of the best representatives, the more saintly types – it could be a local priest, pastor, imam, rabbi, monk or tribal holy man – of a religious community who display a moral purity and inspiringly good character. These individuals may disagree about the correct theology or metaphysics, but their shared morality transcends a concern with doctrinal differences to highlight that perhaps, as Kant maintained, the only thing that ultimately counts is the quality of a person's moral character: the universal aspect of ourselves to which Kant dedicated his life, writings and teaching at the university to help people appreciate and improve.

7

Kant's 'Table Society' and His Battles against a New Era

It took some years before Kant was able to settle down into his own house, but his finances eventually allowed him to purchase a large, two-storey house in the centre of the city on a relatively quiet street near the end of 1783. In his former apartments, he never seemed to get away from the outside noise, leading him to shift from one lodging to the next. When he lived close to the river, the sound of the boats bothered him, and when he lived above Kanter's bookstore, a crowing rooster kept him on edge. The new house was a distinct improvement, although he was still distracted by the singing of the prisoners in the nearby castle prison. To this effect, he could not resist making a comment in his *Critique of the Power of Judgment*:

> Those who have recommended the singing of spiritual songs as part of the domestic rites of worship have not considered that by means of such a noisy (and precisely for that reason usually pharisaical) form of worship they have imposed a great inconvenience on the public, for they have forced the neighborhood either to join in their singing or to give up their own train of thought.[1]

The house was nonetheless excellent for his needs. It was close to the university and contained a room where he could give his lectures. It had a dining area where he could entertain guests, areas for a personal library and a study, a kitchen, an apartment for a cook, a bedroom for himself and an attic where his long-time servant Martin Lampe, a former soldier in the Prussian army, could reside. There was also a small balcony at the back of the house with an attractive garden overlook. Kant could see the steeple of the Löbenicht church from his study, which he always enjoyed contemplating. Impressive and yet modest – he did not decorate it extensively and kept over his desk only a portrait of Jean-Jacques Rousseau – the house was well suited to a full professor at the university with a set of well-connected friends who were often invited over for afternoon meals ('dinner' around 1 p.m., given how Kant arose at 5 a.m. each day). Kant moved in around his sixtieth birthday in early 1784 and remained there until his death twenty years later, in 1804, as he approached the age of eighty.

To those in his community who were aware of his extraordinary intellectual powers, it was always a pleasant surprise how Kant was able to converse entertainingly and interestingly with just about anyone. An excellent host, he invited numerous friends to his home regularly for meals. As he did for everything else in his life, much of which was geared towards maintaining a healthy lifestyle – a sound mind in a sound body, a balance of the intellectual and the sensuous – he reflected at considerable length upon how the social

View of Königsberg Castle, with Kant's house at lower left, *c.* 1835.

interactions during a friendly meal should ideally proceed. He prescribed the best number of people, the kinds of foods, the topics of conversation and the sequence of discussion. In his lectures on anthropology we read the following:

> At a full table, where the number of courses is intended only to keep the guests together for a long time (coenam ducere), the conversation usually goes through three stages: (1) narration, (2) arguing and (3) jesting. – A. The first stage concerns the news of the day, first domestic, then foreign, that has flowed in from personal letters and newspapers. – B. When this first appetite has been satisfied, the party becomes even livelier, for in subtle reasoning it is difficult to avoid diversity of judgment over one and the same object that has been brought up . . . [and so] a dispute arises which stirs up the appetite for food and drink and also makes the appetite wholesome in proportion to the liveliness of this dispute and the participation in it. – C. But because arguing is always a kind of work and exertion of one's powers, it eventually becomes tiresome as a result of engaging in it while eating rather copiously: thus the conversation sinks naturally to the mere play of wit . . . And so the meal ends with laughter, which, if it is loud and good-natured, has actually been determined by nature to help the stomach in the digestive process through the movement of the diaphragm and intestines, thus promoting physical well-being.[2]

Kant's dinner-party rules are usually discussed with either an innocently charming or unqualifiedly supportive tone in appreciation of his effort to formulate the socially ideal way to conduct oneself while eating with other people. And there is indeed some value in his prescription of the ideal get-together. Rule-breaking in general, however, was anathema to him and he had many rules for mealtime behaviour, perhaps too many, among the most stringent of which concerned alcoholic beverages: alcohol loosens the tongue, so a bit of drinking is fine, but one should never, ever get uncontrollably drunk.

Concerning excessive drunkenness, Kant's attitude was harsh: 'A human being who is drunk is like a mere animal, not to be treated as a human being' and is moreover 'below even the nature of an animal'.[3] Within the parameters of his own moral theory, it is puzzling how it could follow reasonably that a person who is excessively drunk would no longer deserve to be treated with the respect that all human beings deserve, as if being treated with respect as a human were not an inalienable right, but could be lost somehow by not having developed or displayed one's rationality sufficiently. Kant recognized all humans as essentially rational beings worthy of respect from the moment of birth – an unqualified egalitarian outlook upon which the beauty and attractiveness of his moral theory rest.

To appreciate this, consider how humans are among the Earth's precious beings, for unlike other animals, and perhaps uniquely, they are reflectively aware of time's passing, the future and the past, their upcoming death, have language, write poetry, laugh and create fine art. Imagine the seedling of a rare medicinal plant, still in its undeveloped stages, perhaps only an inch high. One would not kill the seedling on account of its not having reached maturity, considering its potential. But suppose its death were immanent owing to an upcoming drought or the sudden unavailability of some sustaining nutrients. There still might be resistance to neglecting the seedling or actively throwing it away, simply due to the respect for the kind of being that it is, a respect for its mere existence as such. Intuitively and generally, this is the idea that underlies Kant's moral theory. He states:

> Now I say that the human being and in general every rational being exists as an end in itself, not merely as a means to be used by this or that will at its discretion; instead he must in all his actions, whether directed to himself or also to other rational beings, always be regarded at the same time as an end.[4]
>
> ... For the offspring is a *person*, and it is impossible to form a concept of the production of a being endowed with freedom through a physical operation. So *from a practical point of view*

> it is a quite correct and even necessary idea to regard the act of procreation as one by which we have brought a person into the world without his consent and on our own initiative, for which deed the parents incur an obligation to make the child content with his condition so far as they can.[5]

One way to interpret Kant's condemnation of drunkenness and lapse from his considered moral beliefs is to see it as an expression of his own personal fear of losing control of his fleshly desires, all-too-human in another sense, directly connected with his concern to stay healthy at all costs. From youth, Kant knew that his body was frail. As a matter of maintaining his health, this awareness translated into living according to strict rules and routines in a regulated life of rigorous self-control: he rose early in the morning at the same hour each day, carefully chose his food, prepared his lectures, studied at an appointed time, took a walk in the afternoon for exercise on a daily schedule and carefully managed himself, one can say, to the point of turning himself into a Leibnizian monad, free as a matter of complete self-determination, programming and predictability, as Earth circles the Sun.

Kant might have had a weak body, but he had an iron will that kept his body going for close to eighty years, perhaps too long, given how he suffered at length from old age in his final years. Regularity and consistency were nonetheless aspects of his conception of health as well as his conception of morality. The balance between the sensuous and the intellectual, between body and mind, was also at the basis of his theory of knowledge, so this idea, essentially medical, permeated his entire existence, both practical and theoretical. This is not to say that Kant didn't have plenty of fun and enjoyment with his friends; it is to say that these pleasures were all situated within the self-determined structure of a fixed routine.

We should add that there was an immediate, personal influence on Kant's powerful commitment to a regularly scheduled lifestyle from his friendship with Joseph Green, who was a stickler for punctuality. If one did not keep an appointment with Green to the precise minute, he would simply move on and leave one standing in the dust. As one of Green's close friends whom he saw almost every day, Kant absorbed this attention to timekeeping, which fitted in well with his own medical and self-care concerns. Kant was less disciplined before he met Green and in the long term, that friendship reshaped his lifestyle most beneficially.

Regularity and discipline were also inherent in the spirit of the times. Michel Foucault (1926–1984), the French philosopher and historian of systems of thought, highlights this in his description of how the prevailing conception of a 'soldier' changed from the seventeenth to the eighteenth century. At first, soldiers were 'found': army representatives would enlist the naturally tallest and strongest men from a town or city. Later, however, almost any individual would do, for it was then believed that soldiers could be 'made' through a strict disciplinary regimen:

> By the late eighteenth century, the soldier has become something that can be made; out of a formless clay, an inapt body, the machine required can be constructed; posture is gradually corrected; a calculated constraint runs slowly through each part of the body, mastering it, making it pliable, ready at all times, turning silently into the automatism of habit; in short, one has 'got rid of the peasant' and given him 'the air of a soldier' (ordinance of 2. March 1764).[6]

A memorable exemplar of how soldiering and strict discipline were united is Frederick the Great's military secretary and assistant Friedrich Wilhelm von Steuben (1730–1794), intelligent, talented and courageous, who travelled to North America during the American Revolution to assist George Washington in the training of the Continental Army. Later known as the 'father of the U.S. Army' for having transformed the Continental Army from an undisciplined mob into an organized fighting force, von Steuben wrote the first drill manual for the American troops, detailed and extensive, and eventually rose to become Washington's trusted chief of staff. In him, the Prussian sense of self-discipline travelled across the Atlantic Ocean to help the Americans win their war against

Britain. It might not be too much of an exaggeration to understand Kant's own self-management or 'care of the self' as an artefact of his times, virtually military in its predictability, regimen and effectiveness.

On the lighter side of Kant's dinner rules, there is a fictional depiction of a festive mealtime – Kant is reading a letter to everyone, presumably of some daily news – in *Kant and His Friends at Table* (1892–3), a painting by Emil Doerstling, often reproduced, done close to a hundred years after Kant's death. The people sitting around the table were not all present at the same time in reality, but the collection of individuals tells us about the kinds of friends and acquaintances Kant had. The people around the table (Kant's servant Martin Lampe is standing on the side) are Robert Motherby, English merchant and Kant's long-time friend; Johann Conrad Jacobi, also a merchant and former husband of Maria Charlotta Jacobi, the woman who had invited Kant over to her garden decades before to 'get her watch wound'; Christian Jacob Kraus, professor of practical philosophy, one of Kant's students in earlier years and a close friend in later years, who to an extent took Joseph Green's place; and Johann Georg Hamann, philosopher. Also shown are Johann Georg Scheffner, lawyer, civil servant, soldier, erotic poet and estate owner; Ludwig Ernst von Borowski, a student of Kant when young, later pastor and early biographer of Kant; Karl Gottfried Hagen, pharmacist and professor of medicine; and Theodor Gottlieb von Hippel, police superintendent, the mayor of Königsberg and, when young, author of the play *Der Mann nach der Uhr, oder der ordentliche Mann* (1765; The Man by the Clock; or, the Orderly Man), a work that has been said to portray Kant and his friend Green as living comically and slavishly according to the watch's schedule.

Among those depicted, the friends who regularly visited Kant's house and had meals with him were Motherby, Kraus, Scheffner, Borowski and von Hippel. Kant's best friend Joseph Green wasn't in the painting, although Kant also saw him regularly until Green passed away in June 1786, only two years after Kant moved into his new house. Kant took Green's death hard. After his death, Kant

Emil Doerstling, *Kant and Friends at Table*, 1892–3, postcard of coloured woodcut engraving by Klose & Wollmerstaedt.

withdrew noticeably from socializing in the later part of the day and early evenings – the time when he used to visit Green on most days. Less than two months later, Frederick the Great died as well, a leader whom Kant greatly admired, for a second loss.

Doerstling's fictional painting provides a sampling of Kant's friends and close associates, but it is illuminating to see the full array of professions of the others he invited to his 'table society'. Included were Johann Brahl, newspaper editor; Johann Gottfried Frey, police inspector and war counsellor; Friedrich Conrad Jacobi, Johann's nephew and businessman; Christian Friedrich Jensch, assessor of the city and orphan courts; Johann Christoph Mortzfeldt, medical doctor; William Motherby, Robert's son and medical doctor; Matthias Friedrich Nicolovius, publisher; Christian Friedrich Reusch, lawyer; Friedrich Theodor Rink, professor of oriental languages and Kant biographer; Wilhelm Ludwig Ruffman, bank director; George Michael Sommer, pastor; Johann Friedrich Vigilantius, lawyer; Karl Ludwig Pörschke, professor of philosophy; and Ehregott Andreas Christoph Wasianski, pastor and Kant biographer. We have here in Kant's immediate circle of friends a group of publishers, government administrators, bankers, business people, clergy, professors, lawyers and medical doctors.

His mealtime socializing and numerous friends notwithstanding, Kant's siblings were never part of the picture. By the 1780s Kant had only two sisters remaining, Maria Elisabeth (Krönert, 1727–1796) and Katharina Barbara (Theuer, 1731–1807), neither of whom were educated (they signed their names with an 'X'), and a brother, Johann Heinrich (1735–1800), a pastor living in Alt-Rahden (today, Vecsaule, Latvia), a distant town about 450 kilometres (280 mi.) northeast of Königsberg.

Kant appears to have been conflicted over his relationship with his sisters and brother. Johann wrote to him repeatedly, invitingly and always in an openly friendly way, if sporadically, from the 1760s, but Kant rarely responded. On the few occasions when he did so – once he sent a book on housekeeping to his sister-in-law, which was gratefully received by the family – it was often after months had passed. But Kant's responses to his brother were always caringly worded and apologetic whenever he did write, as infrequent as his letters were. With his sisters he had virtually no personal contact, but still, this did not prevent him from financially looking after them and their families, or his sister Katharina Barbara coming to take care of him compassionately at the end of his life. He provided a pension for his sister Maria from 1768 until her death in 1795, 27 years in total, as well as one for Katharina, and assured his brother that he was taking care of everyone:

> I have not allowed any of my siblings or any of their numerous children (some of whom already have children of their own) to be needy, and I will continue in this way until my own place in the world becomes vacant, at which time I hope to leave something more for my relatives and siblings, a not inconsiderable sum.[7]

When Johann died, Kant also generously helped his sister-in-law and her children, leaving half of his estate to them. For whatever reason, though, he kept a clear separation between himself and his sisters and brother, along with their children, Amalia, Minna, Friedrich Wilhelm and Henriette, who knew him only from a distance and never had the chance to meet their Uncle Immanuel.

This distancing on Kant's part was also an aspect of his personality: given the kinds of friends with which he chose to surround himself, virtually all successful career people, some of whom had considerable influence, his attractive conversational abilities can be compared to those of an extremely likeable, seasoned and successful diplomat, skilled at social gatherings that include administrators, businesspeople, aristocracy, government representatives and other professionals, who knows how to keep his more personal feelings to himself. His biographer E.A.C. Wasianski noted that although he knew Kant for a long time, it took more than a decade for Kant to really open up to him.

Kant's own mealtime get-togethers were inspired by his long-term friendship with Countess Charlotte Caroline Amalie von Keyserling (1727–1791), from whom he learned the art of conversation as a frequent dinner visitor at her palace. Here he had a standing invitation from the countess, sometimes attending her dinners several days in a row, often with a seat next to her. The two were friends for years, similar in age and shared a variety of intellectual interests. She was intelligent, artistic, did translations of works from German into French and at one point did a portrait of Kant.

Among the countess's dinner guests were some of Kant's friends who later attended his own meals, such as von Hippel, Kraus, Mangelsdorff and Scheffner. Kraus had been a tutor to the countess's children earlier on, so there was a familiarity between the Kantian circle of friends and that of the countess – one that continued into the next generation: Johann Georg Hamann's son Johann Michael Hamann, who was also a frequent guest at the palace, became tutor to the children of Caroline's son Albrecht Johann Otto von Keyserling.

Caroline had been connected to power and prestige from the start, for her father was an advisor to King Frederick William I. Her first husband, Gebhardt Johann von Keyserlingk (1699–1761), whom she married at the age of fifteen (he was 44; Caroline was his third wife), was a diplomat, the ambassador to Russia for the duke of Brunswick-Wolfenbuettel. His cousin Hermann Carl von Keyserlingk (1696–1764) was also a quite influential diplomat and director of an embassy, working with the Russian government as well.

After Gebhardt Johann's death, Caroline married Hermann's son, Heinrich Christian von Keyserling (1727–1787), who was the same age as her. Heinrich was a diplomat with both the Russians and the Holy Roman Empire when young and later became one of the wealthiest people in Königsberg. His and his wife's get-togethers included not only Kant and his friends, but Russian officers during the occupation and notable aristocrats.

In sum, when Kant wasn't teaching and doing his intellectual work, he was socializing for years at the highest levels of Königsberg society. Consider the following excerpt from a 1776 newspaper article, which gives an example of the activities at the palace where Kant was spending his time and of Heinrich Christian's impressive social status. It describes the visit of the Grand Duke Paul of Russia and Prince Heinrich of Prussia:

> Dinner was served at the palace by the Russian State Counsellor, Excellency count Heinrich Keyserlingk. After the midday meal the host left with the guests to inspect the fortress of Friedensburg and returned in time for supper. In the meantime the park was illuminated by many thousand lampions and an allegorical design was erected which illustrated the affection between the two high personages. Paul Patrovitch was shown leaning on a palm tree (the Keyserlingk family crest) while the prince of Prussia was supported by a laurel tree. There were two extended hands of the princes and underneath the inscription: 'amitie.' After supper the count guided his guests into the illuminated park.[8]

Doerstling's painting of Kant and his friends at the table gives us a reliable picture of Kant's social circle, but Hamann's inclusion requires some qualification. Only six years apart in age and both from Königsberg, they had known each other since 1759, when Hamann had been working as a business emissary to London for one of Kant's friends, Johann Christoph Berens (1729–1792). While in London, Hamann's mission to the Russian embassy failed embarrassingly and from this followed an overpowering sense of defeat, a subsequent descent into months of intoxication via alcohol and sex, and the squandering of his travel funds from Berens, all of which was topped off with a romantic affair with another man that ended in betrayal and miserable heartbreak for Hamann. Upon reaching the depths of despair and dark night of the soul, as often happens in such cases, Hamann had an indelibly life-changing religious experience wherein he experienced a personal connection with God that revealed to him a new path in life. He dedicated himself thereafter to Bible study and never strayed from a mystically grounded, poetic and devout theistic faith in the decades to come. Although he was not raised as a Pietist, the structure of Hamann's experience was a textbook case of religious conversion as described and advocated by Francke.

Kant probably noticed the Pietistic structure underlying Hamann's transition to a faith in God that transcends reason. Perhaps remembering his own upbringing, he always seemed to be forgiving about Hamann's repeated hostility and resistance to his and Berens's efforts to return him to what they considered to be a more sober perspective – one aligned with the Enlightenment ideal of guiding one's life in reference to reason alone, without leaps of faith into a realm where discussion can gain no foothold and rational justification no longer has a say. To his credit, Hamann had an extraordinarily powerful intellect – not quite as strong as Kant's, as he himself admitted – which Kant surely appreciated. At one point, though, Kant probably realized that it was fruitless to expect a change in Hamann's outlook. His friend – perhaps one could call him that – was a poetically minded visionary who in some of his texts quoted scripture throughout, embellishing and interpreting passages with an overflow of literary imagery, often referring to God in a stream-of-consciousness style. So although Kant and Hamann socialized in the same aristocratic circles for years without apparent difficulty, they never saw eye to eye on philosophical matters or agreed upon the best way to convey truth through written language – either literalistically and logically, as Kant believed, or poetically and imagistically, as did Hamann – and cannot easily be counted as good, trusted friends in a relaxed and open sense, as Doerstling's painting leads us to imagine.

Hamann and Kant are typically portrayed as polar opposites, with Hamann representing the Storm and Stress (*Sturm und Drang*) movement that highlighted the experience of intense feelings and Kant representing the Enlightenment and its commitment to interpreting the world through the lens of pure reason. There is some validity to the contrast. It should be appreciated, though, that both Hamann and Kant were living during the final years of the Enlightenment and that both of their outlooks reflect this. As mystically theistic as he was, Hamann's collective insights proved to be ahead of his time – a kind of spearhead to what was to come in the early nineteenth century. But neither did Kant uncritically accept the scientific and rationalistic world-views that had dominated in the preceding century. Unlike the canonical Enlightenment view that acknowledges reason as a force powerful enough to prove the existence of God and to reveal otherworldly metaphysical realities, Kant denied reason this metaphysical power and gave a more influential role to human activity in experience, far less to God. In this, he stepped forward towards a more down to earth, human-centred philosophical position, despite his unwavering commitment to understanding everything universalistically in terms of pure reason that remains true for all human beings at all times.

Hamann wrote a critique of Kant's philosophy in 1784 entitled 'Metacritique on the Purism of Reason' that aimed to undermine Kant's fundamental assumptions. He did not analyse and refute Kant's specific arguments but attacked the method upon which they were based in a 'metacritique', as he referred to it. The attack fitted with the advancing spirit of the times that was beginning to focus on more down-to-earth realities and leaving behind appeals to otherworldly realities such as God, or, in Kant's case, abstract constructions of pure reason such as 'human nature', whose reality appeared ghostlike. To Hamann, Kant's philosophy was an edifice of false abstractions. Moreover, in the course of playing them out philosophically, it overlooked the living, feeling, concrete reality of actual people. Some decades later, Hegel expressed the same concern about Enlightenment-style thinking:

> 'What is human nature in its purity?' This expression, 'human nature in its purity,' should imply no more than accordance with the general concept. But the living nature of man is always other than the concept of the same, and hence what for the concept is a bare modification, a pure accident, a superfluity, becomes a necessity, something living, perhaps the only thing which is natural and beautiful . . . The universal concepts of human nature are too empty to afford a criterion for the special and necessarily multiplex needs of religious feeling.[9]

These thoughts are part of a larger wave of change that defined the transition from the eighteenth to the nineteenth century, with the replacement of the 'world-as-ticking-watch' analogy that captivated scientific thought during the Enlightenment – and Kant continued to be no exception – with the 'world-as-living-organism' model. With advances in biology and a subsequently closer attention to and identification with the structure of living things as rich, organically unified beings – not to mention frustration with the methods of pure reason, which were seen to generate merely mechanical and emotionally cold understandings of the human being – the ideas of 'life' and 'growth' started to take hold. It was not long before theorists began to understand human history as a growth, or developmental, process, as well as all other specific areas of human life. With closer attention to the human as a concrete, living being, the importance of emotional life also came into the foreground and along with it, an attention to the more instinctual, spontaneous, non-rational aspects of the mind, in particular the unconscious as fountainhead of creativity, poetic inspiration and artistic genius. A new wave of thought emerged at the end of the eighteenth century and Kant found himself in a struggle against

Johann Heinrich Lips, *Johann Georg Hamann*, 1776, engraving.

Anton Graff, *Johann Gottfried Herder*, 1785, oil on canvas.

it, for his love of mathematics and science inextricably wedded him to the image of the physical world as an immense, thoroughly predictable clockwork.

Just as Kant's differences with Hamann are an artefact of this global transition in world-view, the same kind of tension arose between Kant and one of his most talented students, Johann Gottfried Herder. He was a devoted student when attending Kant's lectures, taking notes at length and absorbing Kant's ideas carefully, but he was also an original and energetic thinker. Hamann became one of Herder's teachers and in time, Herder became more substantially influenced by Hamann and his poetically inspired ways. One of the upshots of this dual training was Herder's main work, *Outlines of a Philosophy of the History of Man*, the first volume of which was published in 1784, the same year in which Hamann wrote his metacritique of Kant's philosophy. It was extensive in scope and discussed in his own way many of the themes to which Kant attended over the years, such as the origin of the universe, differences in climate, differences between races, human happiness, art, science, religion and the fate of humanity.

Kant reviewed the first parts of Herder's book in 1785, and it was evident that he was disappointed by Herder's rendition of the many themes upon which he had himself worked so carefully over the years – as we know, Kant had developed a scientifically grounded account of the universe's origins many years before, surpassing Newton, and had been lecturing extensively on anthropology and physical geometry. Herder's version was more poetic, visionary and speculative, riddled with unjustified assertions, as far as Kant could tell. Most annoying was Herder's fundamental postulation of an 'organic force' that was at the basis of everything – an energy that Kant, from the days of his first publication, had denied was mathematically expressible. He reiterated his long-time position in the review:

> Yet what is one to think in general about the hypothesis of invisible forces, effecting organization, hence about the endeavor to want to explain what one does not comprehend from what one comprehends even less? At least with respect to the former we can become acquainted with its laws through experience, although their causes will remain unknown; but with respect to the latter [viz. 'organic force'] we are deprived of all experience, and now what can the philosopher adduce here in justification of his allegation, except the mere despair about ever finding the disclosure in any cognition of nature and the decision he is forced into of seeking for it in the fruitful field of his poetic power? Also this is metaphysics, indeed even a very dogmatic one, however much our writer denies it because that is what the fashion wills.[10]

Although some of the discussions in Herder's book are speculative and implausible in their specifics, he was historically on the right track in terms of understanding the world as governed by the principle of organic unity. It would take someone like Hegel to articulate Herder's vision in a more precise and plausible way, but Herder's book posed a threat to Kant, not unlike what he experienced upon reading Swedenborg years earlier, for in both cases Kant was facing capable, sophisticated thinkers who were explaining things in a manner that he regarded as imprecise and fundamentally wrongheaded in their non-mathematically grounded, less logically governed, more visionary ways.

As one might expect, Kant's review did not sit well with Herder and their friendly relationship dissolved. Despite such a powerful blow from his former teacher, there was something good-natured about Herder's character, for years later he wrote a heartwarming remembrance of Kant in his *Letters on the Advancement of Humanity*:

> I have had the good fortune to know a philosopher. He was my teacher. In his prime he had the happy sprightliness of youth; he continued to have it, I believe, even as a very old man. His broad forehead, built for thought, was the seat of an imperturbable cheerfulness and joy. Speech, the richest in thought, flowed from his lips. Playfulness, wit, and humor were at his command. His lectures were the most entertaining talks. His mind, which examined Leibniz, Wolff, Baumgarten, Crusius, and Hume, and investigated the laws of nature of Newton, Kepler, and the physicists, comprehended equally the newest works of Rousseau . . . and the latest discoveries in science. He weighed them all, and always came back to the unbiased knowledge of nature and to the moral worth of man. The history of men and peoples, natural history and science, mathematics and observation, were the sources from which he enlivened his lectures and conversation. No cabal, no sect, no prejudice, no desire for fame, could ever tempt him in the slightest away from broadening and illuminating the truth. He incited and gently forced others to think for themselves; despotism was foreign to his mind. This man, whom I name with the greatest gratitude and respect, was Immanuel Kant.[11]

Kant's student Jachmann gave a similarly complimentary description of Kant's personal appearance:

> Kant's face had a very pleasant composition, and must have been quite handsome in earlier years. His hair was blond, his

complexion fresh and his cheeks, even in old age, were a healthy red. But how do I find the words to describe to you his eye! Kant's eye was as though made of a heavenly aether from which the deep glance of his soul shone forth, its fiery beam slightly muted by a light cloud. It is impossible to describe the enchanting view, and the feeling this gave me, when Kant would sit across from me with his eyes cast down, and then suddenly raise them and look at me. It was always as if I was looking through this blue aetherial fire into Minerva's inner temple.[12]

Although it is an idealization, for Kant certainly had his flaws, Herder's and Jachmann's accounts, as well as those of others, resonate agreeably with Friedrich Schiller's characterization of the beautiful soul:

> A beautiful soul spreads an irresistible grace over a physique lacking in architectonic beauty and often one even sees it triumph over natural shortcomings. All movements that emanate from it become light and gentle, and yet lively. The eye shines bright and clear, and sentiment gleams in it.[13]

8

The Writings of the 1780s: Kant's Three *Critiques*

When he moved into his new house in 1784, Kant was at the beginning of his most productive decade. One can imagine him sitting upstairs in his study engaged in writing, taking contemplative breaks to gaze upon the Löbenicht Church steeple from his window, the sight of which he treasured so much. There is also the matter of his motivation at this point, for the *Critique of Pure Reason* – a book that had been years in the making and of which he was proud – was dismissed in the first review of the book in early 1782, written in part by J.G.H. Feder (1740–1821), who edited a draft supplied to him by Christian Garve (1742–1798). Feder was a professor of philosophy at the University of Göttingen; Garve was a former professor of logic and mathematics at the University of Leipzig, well known and respected for his translations and scholarly work. The review's opinion was that the *Critique* offered nothing substantial beyond the immaterialist philosophy of Bishop George Berkeley – a philosophy that no one found especially plausible.

Realizing in frustration and annoyance that he was not being understood, Kant used some of his next publications to distinguish his view from Berkeley's. In his *Prolegomena to Any Future Metaphysics*, published in 1783 – a work that was intended to present in a more accessible format and summarize for a wider audience the main ideas of the *Critique of Pure Reason* – he discussed the Garve–Feder review and Berkeley's idealism at some length. That he felt under threat was evident, for the tone of that discussion compared in its persistent sarcasm and condescension to his attacks on Swedenborg and Herder. In the second edition of the *Critique* (1787),

Löbenicht Church, postcard.

Kant enhanced his discussion of Berkeley's idealism in a section called 'refutation of idealism', aiming to show the distinctiveness of his views. As have many of his later commentators, he surely struggled over the years with the accusation that his *Critique* was old Berkeleyan wine in a new Kantian bottle.

Bishop Berkeley was famous for his 'immaterialist' outlook: there are only spirits and their ideas; there is no external, material world that exists as an intermediary between us and God. It is as if we were all spirits in heaven – a view fitting for a bishop – where God communicates with us by coordinating and conveying ideas into each of our minds to give the subjective impression of a public world that we all share. In each of our private mental theatres, we simultaneously watch the same general film, each instance of which God modifies slightly to accommodate our individual perspectives. On this view, what we ordinarily call 'nature' or the 'objective, public, world' are the patterns of ideas that God sends into our minds, nothing more; those ideas contrast with the ones we form for ourselves, allowing a distinction between what is imaginary and subjective as opposed to objective 'nature'.

Since Kant stated that everything of which we are directly aware is 'representations' we construct out of given sensations, it is tempting to regard his view as akin to Berkeley's once we substitute Berkeleyan 'ideas' for Kantian 'representations' and 'God' for Kant's unknowable 'thing-in-itself'. But Kant forcefully resisted this equation. Whether he was convincing in his argument has been a subject of debate among Kant scholars ever since.

Such inconclusiveness notwithstanding, a way to distinguish Kant's view from Berkeley's can be appreciated if we recall a watershed moment in scientific thinking from Galileo Galilei (1564–1642):

> Now I say that whenever I conceive any material or corporeal substance, I immediately feel the need to think of it as bounded, and as having this or that shape; as being large or small in relation to other things, and in some specific place at any given time; as being in motion or at rest; as touching or not touching some other body; and as being one in number, or few or many. From these conditions I cannot separate such a substance by any stretch of my imagination. But that it must be white or red, bitter or sweet, noisy or silent, and of sweet or foul odor, my mind does not feel compelled to bring in as necessary accompaniments. Without the senses as our guides, reason or imagination unaided would probably never arrive at qualities like these. Hence I think that tastes, odors, colors, and so on are no more than mere names so far as the object in which we place them is concerned, and that they reside only in the consciousness. *Hence if the living creature were removed, all these qualities would be wiped away and annihilated* . . . [emphasis added]

> . . . To excite in us tastes, odors, and sounds I believe that nothing is required in external bodies except shapes, numbers, and slow and rapid movements. *I think that if ears, tongues, and noses were removed, shapes and numbers and motions would remain, but not odors or tastes or sounds . . .*[1] [emphasis added]

Galileo distinguished mind-*independent* qualities such as the shapes, movements and quantitative aspects of external things from mind-*dependent* qualities such as colours, tastes, sounds, odours and textures as they are experienced and directly felt. Whereas the mind-independent qualities remain unchanged whether or not we happen to be present and perceiving the objects that have them, the mind-dependent qualities do not exist without the perceivers. If there were no tongues, for instance, 'sweetness' would not exist. In contrast, presumably before living things came into being, the physical Earth was here, extended, filled with shaped objects with measurable movements.

On this scientific picture of the world – assuming theism for a moment – God created the material world with its extended objects, shapes and movements, and when living beings emerged, these extensions, shapes and movements stimulated the living beings' sensory organs to produce the experiences that we refer to as colours, tastes, sounds, odours and textures. If we remove those sense organs from the scene, the mind-dependent qualities disappear, along with the sense organs, while the external world remains.

Intensifying this picture and taking it to a new level, Kant added that space and time (that is, the extensions, shapes and movements) are mind-dependent as well – they are aspects of our own minds – which led him to maintain the following, expanding the already astonishing scope of the Galilean claim about colours, tastes, sounds, odours and textures:

> We can accordingly speak of space, extended beings, and so on, only from the human standpoint. If we depart from the subjective condition under which alone we can acquire outer

> intuition, namely that through which we may be affected by objects, then the representation of space signifies nothing at all.[2]

This leads us to a more Kantian picture: there is a mind-independent being that is the behind-the-scenes source of our sensations, but this being is not extended, or shaped, or moving. It is the mind-independent background for the specific spatio-temporal qualities we experience. Just as in the Galilean picture, the extensions, shapes and movements are the mind-independent background of the experienced qualities of colours, tastes, sounds, odours and textures in this or that given physical object – a background that itself has no colour, taste, sound, odour or texture.

On Kant's view, the mind-independent being would, for example, be the behind-the-scenes source or 'ground' for the sensations from which we construct the pen or cup or tree that we perceive and indeed nature as a whole, but would remain 'in itself', unknowable to us. There is no necessity to equate this mind-independent being with God, as someone might who equates Kant's view with Berkeley's; it is equally possible that God created this mind-independent being – this realm of the pens, cups, trees and mountains as they are unknowably in themselves – as the ground for our sensations, just as on the Galilean model, theistically understood, God created the physical world as an extended, shaped, moving being that exists independently of us.

Truth: *The Critique of Pure Reason*

Kant's greatness as a philosopher can only begin to be appreciated by reading the entirety of his *Critique of Pure Reason*, ideally in the original German, although most translations are fairly reliable. This may be a realistic possibility to only a relatively small number of people, but imagine a Shakespeare scholar working in a language other than English who is unable to read English and knows Shakespeare's work only through translations. Much passes by without the possibility of appreciation.

Critik
der
reinen Vernunft

von
Immanuel Kant
Professor in Königsberg.

Riga,
verlegts Johann Friedrich Hartknoch
1781.

Title page of *Critique of Pure Reason*, 1st edn (1781), published by Johann Friedrich Hartknoch.

Complicating this, the *Critique of Pure Reason* is a lengthy work with multiple layers of daunting argument, even to those who have been trained for years in philosophical studies. Moreover, the *Critique of Pure Reason* – the first of three – is only one of Kant's central writings. The other two *Critiques* approach the first in depth and complexity. Despite the mountain one needs to climb to appreciate Kant's staggering intellectual capabilities and genius, it remains that his main ideas and insights are communicable and understandable, albeit in an elementary form.

The innovative theories of space and time that Kant developed in his inaugural dissertation and imported into the *Critique of Pure Reason* were mentioned in Chapter Six and were alluded to above. One of his main arguments about the nature of space, for example, is this: imagine that one is holding a pen. It is not possible to imagine the pen without also imagining the space in which it is located. One can, however, easily think of the space – and, by extension, space as a whole – without any objects at all, without imagining or including the pen. In this respect, the space in which the pen is located is conceived of as being 'prior' or as conceived in a more basic way than the pen. Generally speaking, if we are to experience any particular object in space, then the space in which it is situated must be 'presupposed' as a condition for knowing that it is there at all.

So it is with time. Imagine the same pen passing through time. It is not possible to imagine the pen passing through time without imagining the time through which it is passing. One can, however, easily think of the time passing and by extension, time as a whole without anything in it, without imagining the pen being there passing through it. The experience of the pen depends upon the time, but the passing time does not depend upon the pen. The relationship is asymmetrical. For Kant, space and time are consequently forms that our experience of the world must presuppose – they are 'conditions' for such experience – universal and necessary for us and hence referred to as knowable a priori. They are forms of our mind that we bring to experience, loosely comparable, as noted, to how a fly brings its prismatic eye to each of its experiences and necessarily experiences a prismatic world thereby.

Yet more profound and penetrating, Kant supplements his theories of space and time by reflecting upon what it means for humans to be essentially rational beings, realizing how this entails that humans are essentially logical beings. As part of our given nature we necessarily think in terms of basic logical relationships such as 'This thing has a certain quality,' translatable into logical phrasing as *S is P*, and 'If this, then that,' translatable into logical phrasing as *If A, then B*. Although these are merely abstract formats in general logic, Kant argued importantly that they are also ways in which we comprehend the world around us: we experience a world with things that have qualities, such as a red pen, and we experience these things as interrelated in terms of cause and effect, as when we write with a normally working, ink-filled pen and expect that the ink will continue to flow onto the page as it did the moment before.

Kant's insight about how this should all be understood at the fundamental level of mental processing can be appreciated if we reflect upon the word 'comprehend': the prefix 'com' means 'together' and 'prehend' means 'to hold'. So to 'comprehend' something means to hold it together. Consider the constantly changing light patterns that take place at the back of one's eyes when one is watching a person twirling a baton. The patterns constantly move without any predictable order. But as we watch the baton twirler and say to ourselves 'baton twirler', we hold together those changing light patterns to give them stability for our understanding. The concept 'baton twirler' functions as a stabilizing device for the sensory input that enters our eyes. Kant realized accordingly a general and important truth: concepts are stabilizing functions. We hold the world together – we *comprehend* it – by applying concepts to our sensory input.

Since everyone for Kant is a rational being and thereby thinks in terms of the same basic logical patterns, he saw that as we do with the forms of space and time, everyone brings these logical patterns to our experience in the form of concepts that organize our given sensations. We all hold the world together in the same way. So, for instance, we organize our given sensations into a set of 'things with qualities' or 'substances' by applying the *S is P* logical form. We also organize those things in terms of causal relationships by applying the *If A, then B* logical pattern. The surprising and unexpected result is that the world we experience in space and time of things in causal relationships – 'nature', as Kant calls it – takes on an appearance that is the product of our own mental activity.

In the *Critique of Pure Reason* Kant asks further about the ultimate source of the stability that concepts such as 'substance' and 'causality' lend to our experience. It is a deep question. In response he made an unexpected, history-shaping claim: the source is our own stable sense of self. If one recalls one's childhood, the experiences of last year and what went on today, there is an awareness that it is exactly the same person, the same individual consciousness or form, that the passing of time has been filling with ever-changing content – a consciousness that has been persisting unchanged throughout the years. It has always been 'me' who has had this flow of experience, no one else, who has been holding it all together for so long. For Kant, this unchanging 'me' – it is the same for everyone who says 'I' to themselves – is at the basis of everything that we hold together in our experience through the application of concepts.

So in this regard – and here we have a thought that significantly influenced later German philosophers such as Hegel – when we experience the external world, we are, in effect, looking into a mirror that is a reflection of our own presence. No matter where we look, whether it is realized or not, we are ultimately and always also looking at ourselves, or at the comprehensive activity of one's stable 'self' or what we call 'I'.

There is indeed a real world behind the appearances we create, then, just as there is a real world behind the prismatic experience of the fly, but how this real world is in itself – metaphysical knowledge in the traditional sense – is something we can never know. In this respect, one of the most important conclusions of Kant's theory of knowledge in the *Critique of Pure Reason* is that, as he stated in the introduction to the second edition, 'I had to deny knowledge [that is, metaphysical knowledge, not scientific knowledge] in order to make room for faith.'[3] In this, he saw the *Critique* as rendering a service to theology insofar as it is 'making it independent of the judgment of dogmatic speculation and in that way securing it against all attacks from such opponents'.[4]

Not only did Kant's theory of knowledge make room for religious faith, it established a solid foundation for scientific investigation, for it implied without exception that every event must be conceived of as having a cause – we cannot avoid thinking in an *If A, then B* manner; it is in our nature to do so – and hence that, in the world of physical appearances, everything for us must be conceived of as mechanically determined and susceptible to scientific investigation, like an immense clockwork. His theory of knowledge guarantees the assumption that the future will be like the past, that the natural laws will always hold and that if we had the intellectual power, the physical workings of nature could be thoroughly understood. Kant thereby rendered compatible two of his leading interests: his faith in God's existence and his love of scientific inquiry.

The second half of the *Critique of Pure Reason* contains some intriguing observations and claims. In the first half Kant shows that knowledge of ultimate reality, or things-in-themselves, is beyond the scope of human sensory experience. In the second half, confirming and reinforcing his conclusions, he adds that aiming to achieve such knowledge through pure reasoning, as traditional rationalist philosophers have done, is futile. As examples, he examines four central questions in metaphysics – whether or not the world has a beginning, whether or not the world is composed of indivisible, simple parts or is infinitely divisible, whether or not there is any freedom and whether or not God exists – and shows that our reason generates equally valid proofs for both sides of each of these questions and is unable to provide decisive answers to any of them. His discoveries of these antinomies of reason, as mentioned earlier, were among the initial motivators for his work on the *Critique of Pure Reason*. He argues further along similar lines that the traditional arguments for God's existence – the ontological argument, the cosmological argument and the teleological argument – are invalid in principle, consistent with his view that there is no way for us ever to be certain whether God exists.

For Kant, our reason is a disposition to know things in their totality. We aim to comprehend as much as we can and, in principle, comprehend everything. Our reflections about ultimate matters consequently lead us to extrapolate beyond the limits of human experience to construct idealizations, or ideas, that represent comprehensive totalities such as 'God', 'Soul' and 'World'. As rational beings, everyone is disposed to do this, and is therefore led to believe that actual realities correspond to these constructions. Kant shows in his *Critique of Pure Reason* that we can never know whether such realities exist – they could be nothing more than illusions as far as we can know, necessary illusions that our mind inevitably constructs – for our rationally constructed ideas that direct us imaginatively towards them refer inaccessibly to what is beyond the possibilities of our knowledge.

Goodness: *The Critique of Practical Reason*

As we have seen, Kant's *Critique of Pure Reason* erects an impenetrable wall between us and the acquisition of metaphysical knowledge of a provable, positive sort, thereby making room for religious faith. This, however, is only preliminary to his wider, primary concern, which is to foster the development of human society towards a more perfect, rational, moral condition. Towards this ideal Kant directed his teaching, especially his lectures on physical geography and anthropology, which served as signposts to his students about aspects of the world that could either hinder or reinforce their moral progress.

For such a project a moral theory is required, which was the subject of the *Critique of Practical Reason* (1788), the prelude to which was Kant's *Groundwork for the Metaphysics of Morals* (1785), followed almost a decade later by an extensive application of his moral theory to law, politics and the virtues in his *Metaphysics of Morals* (1797). These were written with a background interest in moral education – an education that could open people's minds to an aspect of themselves that transcends sensory, pleasure-centred, bodily interests and is the source of human dignity.

With respect to the education of the young, Kant believed that memorable models of virtuous character should be provided – ones that would stimulate a moral consciousness and the recognition of values that are immeasurably greater than any worldly attachments and personal happiness. He gives an example:

> We will, accordingly, first show in an example the mark by which pure virtue is tested and, representing it as set-before, say, a ten year-old boy for his appraisal, see whether he must necessarily judge so of himself, without being directed to it by a teacher.

> One tells him the story of an honest man whom someone wants to induce to join the calumniators of an innocent but otherwise powerless person . . . He is offered gain, that is, great gifts or high rank; he rejects them . . . Now threats of loss begin. Among these calumniators are his best friends, who now refuse him their friendship; close relatives, who threaten to disinherit him (he is not wealthy); powerful people, who can pursue and hurt him in all places and circumstances; a prince who threatens him with loss of freedom and even of life itself. But . . . [he] remains firm in his resolution to be truthful, without wavering or even doubting; then my young listener will be raised step by step from mere approval to admiration, from that to amazement, and finally to the greatest veneration and a lively wish that he himself could be such a man . . . All the admiration, and even the endeavor to resemble this character, here rests wholly on the purity of the moral principle, which can be clearly represented only if one removes from the incentive to action everything that people may reckon only to happiness.[5]

To the same effect Kant offers another example, from Rousseau – the famous 'gallows example' often cited in discussions of Kant's moral theory.[6] A person who is driven by sensory pleasures – it is lust in this case – is given a choice either to live on without engaging further in sexual pleasures for the sake of mere personal gratification or be hanged immediately after satisfying his fleshly desires once more. Kant's answer is that the person would undoubtedly choose to live, indicating that even for those who are dominated by sensory interests, there is a recognition of something more valuable than living for sheer pleasure. He then asks the same person another question, introducing a revealing moral factor:

> whether, if his prince demanded, on pain of the same immediate execution, that he give false testimony against an honorable man whom the prince would like to destroy under a plausible pretext, he would consider it possible to overcome his love of life, however great it may be. He would perhaps not venture to

> assert whether he would do it or not, but he must admit without hesitation that it would be possible for him. He judges, therefore, that he can do something because he is aware that he ought to do it and cognizes freedom within him, which, without the moral law, would have remained unknown to him.[7]

One inspiration for this example is the ancient Greek philosopher Socrates (469–399 BCE), who was known to have a steadfast moral character and who actually did refuse, on the pain of death, to take part in the illegal abduction of a political opponent. Speaking to his friends and disciples while imprisoned unjustly by the state and condemned to death, Socrates describes the episode, as his student Plato (427–348 BCE) relates:

> But when the oligarchy of the Thirty was in power, they sent for me and four others into the rotunda, and bade us bring Leon the Salaminian from Salamis, as they wanted to put him to death. This was a specimen of the sort of commands which they were always giving with the view of implicating as many as possible in their crimes; and then I showed, not in word only but in deed, that . . . I cared not a straw for death, and that my great and only care was lest I should do an unrighteous or unholy thing. For the strong arm of that oppressive power did not frighten me into doing wrong; and when we came out of the rotunda the other four went to Salamis and fetched Leon, but I went quietly home. For which I might have lost my life, had not the power of the Thirty shortly afterwards come to an end.[8]

Resonating with these examples is the biblical story of Job, at first a wealthy, comfortable and happy man, who is put through an ordeal of horrible suffering, both physical and mental, that deprives him of his health, possessions and happiness, all to test whether his faith in God can be shaken. In the end it is not, and Job's character is judged to be pure. Since Job has proven himself to be worthy of happiness, God restores his fortunes, giving him twice as much as he had before.

These examples show that Kant's moral stance has a deep-seated, intuitive appeal to our sense of human respect and dignity. We respect people who hold firmly to their beliefs despite threats of physical pain and loss, those who, for instance, refuse to betray under torture or the threat of death their religious beliefs, their country, or their friends and family. The beliefs need not be moral beliefs per se; involved here is a general respect for a person's strength of character and for extraordinary resolve strong enough to admit the sacrifice of personal happiness – or life.

Within the moral context, Kant's examples draw attention to our consciousness of moral demands – demands that we respect and recognize as our duty – that have nothing to do with preserving our happiness, and indeed, embody a value and a dignity that surpasses the importance of our bodily desire to continue living as long as we can. He regards this moral awareness as a fact that any reflective person will recognize as an essential aspect of themselves. It is accompanied by an awareness of one's freedom, which must be presupposed to make sense of feeling responsible for our actions, as we choose to act either in accord or in conflict with what duty requires.

Since moral awareness and the accompanying recognition of our freedom, along with the feeling of responsibility and respect for duty that follow from it, are independent of sensory interests, Kant locates the basis of this awareness in an aspect of ourselves that is itself independent of the spatio-temporal world – an 'intelligible' dimension where our true sense of personhood as someone with the capacity for free choice resides. For Kant, this is also where our rationality resides, and he accordingly develops a moral theory based on reason alone, the centrepiece of which is the absolute moral command to behave in a consistent manner, as opposed to acting inconsistently or illogically. This is the 'categorical imperative (that is, absolute command)', which says to act only such that the rule underlying one's action could serve as a law for everyone.

As discussed earlier, one of Kant's familiar examples is whether it is morally permissible to tell a lie when under duress (or for any other reason). In this case, the rule or 'maxim' underlying such an action can be seen to undermine itself, for if it were universally adopted, trust between people would dissolve and lying would become futile. Since the rule self-destructs, revealing itself to be irrational thereby, we ought not to tell lies. Our duty to be honest is thus simply a matter of acting rationally, which is a matter of respecting ourselves as rational beings. Kant gives other examples as well, such as the duty to not commit suicide, the duty to develop one's talents and the duty to help others in need. Throughout his moral writings he reiterates these examples.

Of particular note is Kant's concern with honesty, which he introduces in a variety of contexts, more than one might expect. An example within his moral theory is how he illustrates the distinction between acting merely 'in accord with' what duty requires as opposed to acting 'from' a respect for duty. He asks us to consider a businessperson who acts honestly but does so only out of self-interest. Here, the businessperson acts in accord with what duty requires, but the actions have no moral worth because the underlying motivation is selfish. A good will does not stand behind them, which for Kant is the only thing in the world that is good without qualification. The businessperson displays a false honesty, inherently deceptive, for had self-interest called for acting dishonestly, that path would have been chosen.

When he was young, Kant's family was in the harness-making business, and from what he said about his parents' good character and their associated religiosity, it is likely that his family conducted its business honestly, setting a memorable moral example. In later years, Kant showed no sympathy to businesspeople who condoned dishonesty, making unforgiving comments about them in his anthropology lectures. There was something about Kant that led him to value honesty as a premium in the estimation of character, for he despised liars, referring to them as 'worthless' in their failure to respect themselves as rational beings.

A widely accepted moral idea is that 'ought implies can', which means that if I ought to do something, it must be possible for me to do it. For example, since I was not alive at the time, it would be absurd for someone to say that I ought to have stopped the assassination of Abraham Lincoln, much as I wish that I could have. The idea sounds obvious, but Kant obtains a great deal of mileage out of it, realizing that if we have an absolute duty to keep our promises, not commit suicide, develop our talents or help others in need – that we unconditionally 'ought' to do these things – then we require the time morally to perfect ourselves, given how we are imperfect beings filled with worldly desires that interfere with our efforts to act morally. Regarding that imperfection, Kant sometimes characterizes people in general as depraved beings, echoing how the Pietists described everyone as in need of being saved from their worldly desires and attachments. Kant concludes that as a condition for the realization of our duties, it is necessary to postulate the continuation of our person – our intelligible self – into the endless future. The immortality of the soul thus emerges as a postulate that follows from the demands of morality.

Furthermore, Kant realizes that there is no logical connection between doing our duty and being happy. 'Morals is not properly the doctrine of how we are to *make* ourselves happy but of how we are to become *worthy* of happiness,' he says.[9] Suppose for a moment, though, that we always acted according to what duty requires. This would not imply that we would be happy. Indeed, Kant notes that when we do our duty, it is often accompanied by frustration insofar as the demands of duty conflict with our desire for comfort. He even states that the moral worth of the action done from duty becomes more distinct and appreciable when we actively turn away from our ordinary sensory desires and experience a measure of frustration.

Nonetheless, the 'highest' good is an ideal condition where everyone who has done their duty gets what they deserve in connection to their sensory interests, namely, the satisfactions of their desires, which is happiness. Since morality and happiness are not logically linked, the realization of the highest good can be guaranteed only if an external power ensures their coordination. For Kant, this can only be God, conceived of as a holy and beneficent author of the world.

In sum, the idea of 'ought implies can' entails the moral postulate of the immortality of the soul and the idea of the highest good entails the moral postulate of God's existence. These are not formal 'proofs' in the sense of logical or scientific proofs. They are 'postulates' necessary to make full sense of our moral awareness. Everything depends upon how much reality we accord to our direct awareness of the moral law, the 'fact of reason', as Kant calls it, and he is certain that it is no illusion. Although there is no logical argument for God's existence and the immortality of the soul along traditional metaphysical lines, Kant regards his moral reasoning based on the reality of morality and freedom that postulates the immortality of the soul and the existence of God as powerful enough to support a rational faith. And once religion is brought into the picture within the context of that faith, it becomes possible to interpret our moral duties in theological terms as divine commands.

Regarding his direct awareness of the moral law, Kant states the following, first famously in the conclusion to the *Critique of Practical Reason* and then, second, in *Religion Within the Bounds of Mere Reason*:

> Two things fill the mind with ever new and increasing admiration and reverence, the more often and more steadily one reflects on them: the starry heavens above me and the moral law within me. I do not need to search for them and merely conjecture them as though they were veiled in obscurity or in the transcendent region beyond my horizon; I see them before me and connect them immediately with the consciousness of my existence.[10]

> Yet there is one thing in our soul which, if we duly fix our eye on it, we cannot cease viewing with the highest wonder, and for which admiration is legitimate and uplifting as well. And that is the original moral predisposition in us, as such.[11]

Such is the general import of Kant's moral theory. He restricted knowledge to make room for faith in his first *Critique* and, with that opening, explained in his second how our moral awareness implies an 'intelligible' aspect of ourselves that transcends the world of sensory desires and spatio-temporal appearances – an intelligible

Karl Wingender, *Friedrich Heinrich Jacobi*, *c.* 1830, oil on canvas.

After Carl Jäger, *Gotthold Ephraim Lessing*, *c.* 1868–78, photographic reproduction.

aspect that he conceived of morally as having a variety of religious implications, the most important of which is rational faith in God's existence.

Kant advocated this moral idea of a rational faith in a 1786 publication, 'What Does It Mean to Orient Oneself in Thinking?', that contributed to what became known as the pantheism controversy – a dramatic debate that permeated German intellectual life during the 1780s and eventually precipitated the rise of post-Kantian philosophy in the writings of J. G. Fichte (1762–1814), F.W.J. Schelling (1775–1854) and G.W.F. Hegel (1770–1831). It began with a challenge by Friedrich Heinrich Jacobi (1743–1819) to the reputation of Gotthold Ephraim Lessing (1729–1781), playwright, philosopher and literary critic, who was one of the great representatives of the German Enlightenment. Jacobi revealed to Lessing's (and Kant's) friend Moses Mendelssohn, who was in the midst of preparing a celebratory manuscript on his recently deceased colleague, that Lessing was an advocate of what was believed at the time to be an atheistic, freedom-denying, heretical outlook to be shunned at all professional and reputational costs: Spinozism, as expressed by Baruch Spinoza (1632–1677), the rationalist and radical Jewish philosopher who lived in Amsterdam and who was excommunicated by the Portuguese Jewish community.

Jacobi interpreted Spinoza's philosophy to be the epitome and logical culmination of the philosophical employment of reason and implied through his association of Spinoza with Lessing the general proposition, threatening to all Enlightenment thinkers, that reason leads eventually and extremely to atheism, fatalism and the utter loss of religious values and faith – hence the emergence of the controversy. For Jacobi, faith is not a rational matter at all but is antithetical to reason; it is an immediate awareness of the world before us and, most importantly, a commitment to God's existence that can only be achieved through a non-rational *salto mortale* or 'leap of faith'.

Mendelssohn defended his friend Lessing from Jacobi's charge in addition to stating his own belief that reason can demonstrate

Unknown artist, *Baruch Spinoza*, 1675–1750, oil on canvas.

God's existence and justify religious values. In his contribution to the controversy, Kant, who was called upon by different parties to defend both Jacobi and Mendelssohn, took a middle ground where he expressed his own position – one that defends the rational faith in God as a necessary postulate of practical reason, as described earlier. He thereby rejected outright Jacobi's non-rational leap of faith as an objectionable and dangerous 'enthusiasm' that opens the door to all kinds of belief, somewhat to Jacobi's dismay, and accepted Mendelssohn's promotion of reason with the important qualification that Mendelssohn had erred in having been too confident about reason's ability to provide us with certainty about metaphysical realities such as God's existence.

Hence followed his own more tempered presentation of how the demands of morality lead us necessarily to a rational faith in the immortality of the soul, God and the highest good as postulates. In the same year as Kant's response to the controversy, Karl Leonhard Reinhold (1757–1823) published an accessible, more popularized presentation of Kant's position in his *Letters on the Kantian Philosophy* where he emphasized Kant's standpoint in the pantheism controversy with the result that Kant's reputation quickly spread. Jacobi's accusations did not come to an end, however. A decade later he levelled the same atheistic charges against Fichte, whom he recognized as Kant's intellectual heir, and by implication against Kant, in what became known as the atheism controversy.

Beauty, Sublimity and Living Things: *The Critique of the Power of Judgment*

Kant had a strong disposition towards scientific studies accompanied by an underlying inclination to philosophical thought, so it is likely that he did not major in theology when he was at the university, just as one of his fellow students reported. Nonetheless, religious concerns had a long-term effect upon his intellectual development. As we have seen, Franz Albert Schultz, the local pastor and Kant's mother's friend when Kant was young, assisted with Kant's entry into a Pietist school and later became a professor of theology at the University of Königsberg and Kant's university colleague throughout the years. In addition, Kant was always a theist. Moreover, his outlook on the world can be seen to have a Pietist structure similar to that of August Hermann Francke, one of the leading Pietist figures. They both believed that as a rule, most people's lives are dominated by pleasure-seeking and self-interest and that there is consequently a need to raise the consciousness of the general public to a more spiritual level conducive to a better society. It is striking how Kant believed that a life of pleasure-seeking is literally worthless:

> It is easy to decide what sort of value life has for us if it is assessed merely by what one enjoys (the natural end of the sum of all inclinations, happiness). Less than zero: for who would start life anew under the same conditions, or even according to a new and self-designed plan (but one still in accord with the course of nature), which would, however, still be aimed merely at enjoyment?[12]

Francke's view was that a better society could be achieved through a radical rebirth of the personality reinforced by Bible study. For Kant, this approach was far too crude in its lack of argumentation and, as such, ineffective in its power to convince serious thinkers. As an Enlightenment-style philosopher of extraordinary sophistication, Kant set aside ritualistic, scriptural and contingent differences between religions, not to mention their various unprovable speculations about the nature of ultimate reality, and attended to what he regarded as the common, real-life essence of religion, moral awareness. In this respect, he had the same goal as the church pastors – Kant's brother was a pastor and they shared the same vocation in this sense – except that he expressed it in an elaborately constructed, extensively argued philosophical theory and a pedagogical programme. When seen from this angle, Kant was in closer spiritual company with Bishop George Berkeley and Father Nicolas Malebranche than one would otherwise imagine. Hence was the goal of his lectures on anthropology and physical geography in the pragmatic sphere and within his philosophical theory, the task of complementing his first two *Critiques* with a third, the *Critique of the Power of Judgment* – a work that explains how the experiences of beauty, sublimity and living organisms can bridge the gulf between the intelligible world of morality and the sensory world of nature within which we are obliged to do our duty.

From the British empiricist tradition in aesthetics, Kant inherited a problem that loomed large in the eyes of theorists such as Edmund Burke (1729–1797) and David Hume (1711–1776): 'Can it make sense to dispute, or argue over, judgments of taste?' The negative answer is expressed in the Latin dictum *De gustibus non disputandum est* (there is no disputing about taste). And yet people argue all the time about whether this wine is good; in art, whether this painting is a masterpiece; or in the natural world, whether these particular flowers are beautiful.

Burke's and Hume's answer to the question was yes, tastes can be disputed to a point, recognizing how people's sense organs tend to operate similarly. For those with healthy sense organs, sugar is sweet, vinegar is sour, unsweetened cocoa is bitter, blue and orange when set next to each other in a painting create a vibrant effect, and so on. This suggests that an ideal condition of the sensory organs can be postulated that could be used as the standard of taste and referred to for settling disputes.

There is a problem, though, for even among those with the most delicately discriminating and apparently healthiest sensory organs, there is no guarantee of agreement. There is no clearly definable and useable ideal upon which to rely in subtle cases, which are usually the important and controversial ones. Consider a well-known example from Hume:

> It is with good reason, says Sancho to the squire with the great nose, that I pretend to have a judgment in wine: this is a quality hereditary in our family. Two of my kinsmen were once called to give their opinion of a hogshead, which was supposed to be excellent, being old and of a good vintage. One of them tastes it; considers it; and after mature reflection pronounces the wine to

> be good, were it not for a small taste of leather, which he perceived in it. The other, after using the same precautions, gives also his verdict in favour of the wine; but with the reserve of a taste of iron, which he could easily distinguish. You cannot imagine how much they were both ridiculed for their judgment. But who laughed in the end? On emptying the hogshead, there was found at the bottom, an old key with a leathern thong tied to it.[13]

There may be no commonly shared ground for judgements of taste in connection with wines, colours, odours, textures and sound qualities, but Kant thought that judging an object's pure beauty had an altogether different basis. Rather than appealing to an ideal condition of our sensory organs – one not clearly definable in any case – to provide a stable reference for our judgements of beauty and explain why we argue about taste, Kant appreciated that unlike our sensory organs, everyone has exactly the same basic cognitive structure that organizes experience in space and time. His *Critique of Pure Reason* explained in detail how this works. So if we attend exclusively to the qualities of an object that are attuned to this common structure, viz., an object's spatio-temporal form, and make a judgement about how our immediate apprehension of the structure makes us feel, there would be a shared ground – indeed a necessary and universal one – to which everyone could refer equally in their estimations and disputes about beauty. It might not settle the disputes, but everyone would at least be referring to their shared, identical mental structure in their discussions and not talking past each other.

For Kant, then, the beauty of an object resides in how the object's spatio-temporal structure makes us feel when we apprehend it. It is a matter of feeling, but it is not a sensory feeling. It is a non-sensory cognitive feeling that is centred in a different part of the mind. The structure of a snowflake is highly organized, for instance, almost as if its organization had a kind of intelligence behind it. It looks like it was designed. The same is true of beautiful crystal formations, flowers and seashells. It is also true of the structure of beautiful buildings such as the Taj Mahal. The structure of this building may have been intelligently and intentionally designed by Ustad Ahmad Lahori (*c.* 1580–1649), but there is also something additionally aesthetically satisfying about its structure, an attractive *je ne sais quoi*, as if it originated from an indefinable and mysterious *natural* intelligence in the architect's mind. In reference to this, one can say that 'nature' is responsible for the additionally pleasing quality of the structure, as it is for the snowflakes and flowers. One may call it Ustad's genius or a source of intelligent inspiration that flows into his consciousness, almost out of nowhere, independently of his intentions and planning.

In these examples, the impressively rational, systematic organization of an object's spatio-temporal structure appeals to our cognitive interests, for an object with an exceptionally impressive rational structure produces the pleasurable feeling that nature was made for our understanding and that in terms of acquiring knowledge of nature, we are perhaps more at home in the world than we first imagined. As such, the feeling of pure beauty applies directly to our interest in formulating a system of scientific knowledge. It can be called an 'aesthetic confirmation' of our scientific interest. Equally if not more so, the feeling applies to our moral interest in doing our duty, for the latter is none other than acting in the material world rationally according to a system of moral laws – a world wherein the system of natural laws, we hope, would be receptive. So Kant's view is that the feeling of pure beauty upon apprehending the systematic structure of an object reinforces our confidence in both scientific advancement and the concrete realization of morality.

With respect to morality, Kant adds that the structure of judgements of pure beauty is supportively analogous to the very structure of moral judgements. Both kinds of judgement give pleasure with the claim for agreement of everyone else, that is, are universalistic, and both raise our consciousness above mere sensory pleasure and interests into the realms of understanding and reason. Given their similar structure, Kant maintains that developing the ability to appreciate pure beauty, especially as it appears in nature, readies the mind for making moral judgements. Pure beauty thereby has a morally educative value, which is one of Kant's main concerns as a philosopher and educator.

The experience of the sublime serves the same end. When we apprehend overwhelmingly large objects or environments such as the Pyramids in Egypt, the interior of St Peter's Basilica in Rome, a range of towering mountains, the Grand Canyon, a vast desert, the apparently endless ocean or the evening sky filled with stars, the idea of infinity comes to mind. In the sphere of natural objects and environments, it is almost as if there were an underlying intellect that is directing us to contemplate the infinite – an idea often associated with God. But this idea of infinity, Kant observes, cannot be fully grasped within the realm of sensory experience. When we try, our imaginations run out of energy, so to say, as we try to extend our imagination to the end of infinite space. And yet, the frustration inherent in this immediately perceptual approach to infinity stirs us to become aware of how we can nonetheless *conceive* of infinity, which reveals a different part of our mind – the purely intellectual part – that transcends the limits of imagination and the sensory world. Becoming aware of that part of the mind, our reason, opens our awareness to the non-sensory, purely rational, seat of morality. In this respect, the experience of the sublime associated with great magnitudes – the 'mathematical' sublime – brings to light our moral awareness.

This moral effect occurs not only in relation to extremely large objects, but in relation to extremely powerful objects or environments such as Niagara Falls:

> Bold, overhanging, as it were threatening cliffs, thunder clouds towering up into the heavens, bringing with them flashes of lightning and crashes of thunder, volcanoes with their all-destroying violence, hurricanes with the devastation they leave behind, the boundless ocean set into a rage, a lofty waterfall on a mighty river, etc.[14]

The experiences of such overwhelmingly powerful phenomena generate the idea that, as physical beings, our lives are fragile and finite. If we get too close to these phenomena, we might not survive. Like the thought of infinity, this experience of the 'dynamical' sublime discloses an aspect of ourselves – our rational aspect – that transcends sensory interests.

We have already seen this kind of experience in Kant's moral theory, as when Socrates defied death threats in his identification of a more valuable aspect of himself that transcends his physical finitude. This was his moral awareness and the accompanying obligation to do what is right. Similarly stimulating such an awareness is the apprehension of overwhelmingly powerful objects or environments that pose an implicit death threat. One could say that it is almost as if the life-threatening phenomena were put there intentionally to raise us to a higher level of self-consciousness, given how purposive they are to our moral interests.

In these reflections, it helps to take note of how the idea of 'purpose' is central. With respect to living things, Kant believed that mechanistic physics, at least as far as we will ever be able to tell, is forever unable to explain the presence of life on earth. He held to this belief from his first publication *Thoughts on the True Estimation of Living Forces* (1747) to the *Critique of the Power of Judgment* (1790). Mechanistic physics regards natural phenomena as components of an immense mechanism governed by cause-and-effect relationships, like a gigantic watch. But a watch is very different from a living organism that grows, reproduces and has a structure where each part depends upon and is sustained by the others, for when part of a watch breaks, the watch does not repair itself or grow a replacement part. An often-cited quote from Kant expresses how he believed physics is inadequate to understand the living quality of living things:

> For it is quite certain that we can never adequately come to know the organized beings and their internal possibility in accordance with merely mechanical principles of nature, let alone explain them; and indeed this is so certain that we can boldly say that it would be absurd for humans even to make such an attempt or to hope that there may yet arise a Newton who could make comprehensible even the generation of a blade of grass according

> to natural laws that no intention has ordered; rather, we must absolutely deny this insight to human beings.[15]

Kant referred to living things as 'natural purposes' insofar as they can only be conceived of as the product of an intelligent design in a manner different from mechanical relationships. It is not as if we could ever know that there is an intelligent designer at the basis of living things, but Kant argues that this is the only way we can make sense of them.

He concludes that to conceive of the possibility of life, it is necessary to assume the intention of an intelligence operating behind the natural scenes. This assumption leads quickly to the question, 'What, then, is the purpose, or ultimate intention, of life on earth?' We can envision here the progression of complexity in living things from one-celled organisms to plants, fish, amphibians, reptiles, birds and mammals. At the top of this hierarchy stand the human beings, the only beings on Earth that have the ability to reason and think morally. This ability distinguishes human beings from all other living things, for the basis of our moral awareness transcends nature and is unconditional in its absolute moral commands. In this regard, Kant states that 'that which has the end of its existence in itself, [is] the *human being*, who determines his ends himself through reason', and that the human being 'is the ultimate end of the creation here on earth, because he is the only being on earth who forms a concept of ends for himself and who by means of his reason can make a system of ends out of an aggregate of purposively formed things'.[16]

By reflecting upon the nature of living things, we are led to appreciate our moral awareness as not only situated outside the mechanistic determinations of nature, but in view of it, an understanding of ourselves as the ultimate meaning of the very system of living things. The intelligent designer that our minds cannot avoid assuming at the basis of nature must be conceived of as having created nature as the place for our moral development. Again, this is no proof that such a designer exists. Kant speaks merely of the only way we can make sense of the presence of living things. Within the sphere of this assumption, he maintains that without the existence of human beings, the sensory world of inanimate nature and living things would be meaningless, echoing how he judges human lives to be meaningless that are centred exclusively on sensory pleasure-seeking:

> If it thinks over the existence of the things in the world and the existence of the world itself, even the most common understanding cannot reject the judgment that all the many creatures, no matter how great the artistry of their arrangement and how manifold the purposive interconnections by which they are related to each other may be, indeed the whole of so many systems of them, which we incorrectly call worlds, would exist for nothing if there were not among them human beings (rational beings in general), i.e., the judgment that without human beings the whole of creation would be a mere desert, existing in vain and without an ultimate meaning.[17]

It may be surprising to see that despite its philosophical sophistication and argumentative detail, Kant's position echoes how the Book of Genesis describes the creation of the world, where human beings are placed by an intelligent creator at the summit of nature and hierarchy of living things. The crucial difference – and Kant emphasizes this repeatedly – is that this view cannot be proven as a metaphysical fact. At best, we can say that this is simply the only way our minds can make sense of the world, which is to say that it proves nothing about the actual existence of an intelligent designer.

In sum, the culminating text of Kant's critical philosophy, the *Critique of the Power of Judgment*, has a unified purpose in his seemingly dissimilar discussions of beauty, sublimity and living organisms. All three lead us to appreciate our moral awareness and how they together form a bridge between the mechanistically conceived natural world and the rational seat of morality that resides beyond it in the realm of pure intelligibility.

9
The Final Years

The events of the year 1789 reverberated profoundly into world history, for Europe saw one of its most powerful, long-standing monarchies overthrown for the first time in favour of a republican government, spreading panic among the aristocracies in the surrounding nations. Facing a major financial crisis, the French king Louis XVI did his best to control and resolve the emergency, but to no avail: political tensions developed to a breaking point where he had little choice but to transfer power over to a governing body that represented the majority of the people. Whereas the change was at first inspirational, it took only a few years before the new government – one that went through a series of increasingly dictatorial transitions as the revolutionary aims became ever more endangered – dissolved the monarchy and in 1793 executed the king and queen, who were intent upon regaining their power.

As did most people in Europe, Kant attentively followed the unfolding of the French Revolution and reflected upon its historical significance. A year after it started, he received a detailed letter from his student Johann Benjamin Jachmann, who was in France at the time and explained how the situation was slowly unravelling:

> My first impression was that I was in the land of the blessed; for all the people, even the lowliest inhabitants, seemed to show by words and deeds that they felt as though they were living in a land that had totally thrown off the yoke and oppression of the mighty, a land where freedom and the rights of mankind were universally honored and cherished to the highest degree . . .

> But this spirit seemed to reign only as long as the people were entertained with celebrations, dances, and banquets that buoyed them up with false promises. As soon as these were discontinued and the deputies from the provinces had drawn back, one heard complaints and discontent expressed from all sides, even from those who had declared themselves to be true friends of the revolution . . . It is the rabble and one or two agitated heads that rule France at present. I have visited the National Assembly myself several times and seen the Assembly compelled to draw up certain decrees, because nobody was allowed to raise the slightest objection to them without being insulted by the rabble on the public rostrum and denounced as a 'aristocrat' . . . Nobody dares to predict what the ultimate outcome of all this will be.[1]

In his estimation of the French Revolution, Kant was of two minds. The initial 1789 power shift he interpreted as legitimate, understanding that Louis XVI had willingly transferred his power over to the people's representatives. This was consistent with his view that political change should always take place *within* the system, no matter how morally repugnant the existing system might be. He was a staunch reformist as opposed to a revolutionist. Working for reform within the system was always preferable to its violent overthrow, for the latter would immediately plunge the society into an animalistic, retrogressive, lawless state of nature devoid of justice where anything could happen.

When the French government became more dictatorial and murderously overthrew the monarchy, however, Kant regarded this as a lawless act and condemned the violence, as he stated in the *Metaphysics of Morals* (1797). Despite this, not too long thereafter, in *The Conflict of the Faculties* (1798), upon taking the longer view of human history, he considered the French Revolution a major social advance insofar as it institutionalized the social ideals of rationality and equality, at least in principle, as stated in the 1789 'Declaration of the Rights of Man and of the Citizen' written with the help of Thomas Jefferson by the Marquis de Lafayette, Abbé Sieyès and

Honoré Mirabeau. Kant regarded these revolutionary ideas as confirming a moral predisposition in humanity – a disposition that he projected would someday be realized in a world federation of free states, as described in his essay 'Perpetual Peace' (1795).

With the death of Frederick the Great in 1786, the political atmosphere in Prussia changed with the ascension of his nephew, Frederick William II (1744–1797). Frederick William had much to his credit as king – he significantly lightened the tax burdens on the people and consciously moved the society away from Frederick the Great's love of French culture to a more Germanic focus – but in 1788 he also instituted a policy that required everyone publicly to profess only the so-called 'genuine' Christianity derived strictly from the Bible, prohibiting attacks, for example, on biblical revelation. From this followed the persecution and censorship of those who did not comply. Among the many who were subject to this kind of censorship in the former home of religious toleration were Kant himself and the young and upcoming scholar Johann Gottlieb Fichte.

Fichte became one of the most influential philosophers of the early nineteenth century, but he had a difficult start and a stormy career. Given his conflict-engendering personality, he tended to gravitate into disagreement with his employers, often losing his job. Nonetheless determined to succeed as a philosopher, he visited Kant as a young man in 1791, hoping to gain his favour and assistance. Having read Kant's moral theory while employed as a tutor, he was convinced that Kant was the greatest thinker alive.

When Fichte visited Kant for the first time – he was 29 and Kant was 67 – the meeting was perfunctory and it seemed as if Kant remained unimpressed and tired. Not discouraged, Fichte went immediately to work on a manuscript in Kant's style and within a few weeks presented to him *Attempt at a Critique of All Revelation* for his professional judgement. Destitute, Fichte also asked Kant for a loan to help him continue his travels. Kant did not provide the loan, but he recommended Fichte's manuscript to his publisher, where it was accepted in principle with an accompanying payment, thereby helping Fichte financially through more respectable means.

But there was an immediate roadblock: the manuscript still needed to pass through the religious censor. It was at first rejected, but with a fortunate change in censor it was accepted and published anonymously, possibly to help with Fichte's public recognition. The manuscript was so similar in style to Kant's own writing that it was at first assumed to be Kant's next book and was initially discussed as such. Upon Kant's revelation that Fichte was the author, Fichte's scholarly career took off. Kant helped him further to attain a position as a tutor and a professorship at the University of Jena followed three years later, where Fichte developed his own philosophical standpoint, original and different from Kant's. In Fichte's mind, he was merely a faithful devotee who was bringing to fruition the logical development and completion of Kant's ideas, although Kant was never a fan of anyone who claimed to be doing this.

Whereas Kant was a thinker who drew compartmentalized divisions between the various areas of inquiry, constructing a philosophy with sharp divisions all around like the joints of a marionette, Fichte sought unity across the board, consistent with

Albrecht Fürchtegott Schultheiß, *Johann Gottlieb Fichte*, c. 1810, print.

the changing spirit of the times that was moving away from the world-as-mechanical-watch analogy to a world-as-living-organism model. Among his new ideas, he sowed the seeds of an innovative kind of logic – a dialectical logic of opposition and reconciliation – that became paramount in Hegel's and, later, Marx's philosophies. Inspired by Kant's moral theory, he also accentuated the idea of 'will' that became central to the thought of Friedrich Nietzsche and Arthur Schopenhauer (1788–1860), who attended Fichte's lectures in Berlin.

When Fichte's philosophy became widely discussed after the 1794 publication of his *Foundations of the Science of Knowledge* (*Wissenschaftslehre*) – a book that presented itself as the next stage of Kant's critical philosophy – Kant initially kept his distance from the discussion. In 1798 Kant and Fichte were still corresponding cordially, although Fichte mentioned to Kant that he was hearing criticisms of his view stemming from Kant's remarks to others, which obviously bothered him, given his respect for Kant. Finally, though, in 1799, motivated by a challenge in a book review that described Fichte as the first true transcendental philosopher who had been able to realize more effectively the ideas that Kant proposed in his *Critique of Pure Reason*, Kant responded publicly with his view of Fichte's work. He dismissed it and denied all connections:

> I hereby declare that I regard Fichte's Wissenschaftslehre as a totally indefensible system. For pure theory of science is nothing more or less than mere logic, and the principles of logic cannot lead to any material knowledge, since logic, that is to say, pure logic, abstracts from the content of knowledge; the attempt to cull a real object out of logic is a vain effort and therefore something that no one has ever achieved. If the transcendental philosophy is correct, such a task requires a passing over into metaphysics. But I am so opposed to metaphysics, as defined according to Fichtean principles, that I have advised him, in a letter, to turn his fine literary gifts to the problem of applying the Critique of Pure Reason rather than squander them in cultivating fruitless sophistries.[2]

Kant published his repudiation of Fichte in August 1799, which could only have exacerbated Fichte's turbulent year. While at the University of Jena in 1798, after having published an essay entitled 'On the Ground of Our Belief in a Divine World-Governance' wherein he stated that 'the moral order is what we are assuming to be *divine*' and that the 'living and active moral order is itself God; we require no other God and can grasp no other,'[3] he was accused of atheism and, by Jacobi, nihilism, precipitating what became known as the atheism controversy. Fichte denied the charges, but reactions were heated and written exchanges in 1799 between him, the government and the university advanced to a point where, although only mildly reprimanded in the end, he was obliged to resign during the summer, after which point he left for Berlin in June 1799, a city which at the time did not have a university of its own.

Kant published the letter that distanced himself from Fichte right after Fichte lost his job. Given Fichte's unshakeable philosophical commitment that morality is the most important thing in the world – one upon which he based his entire career, not unlike Kant – the contents of Kant's letter, not to mention its timing, must have hurt Fichte deeply. Dedicated nonetheless to his philosophical calling, he continued to publish important work in the following years and when the University of Berlin opened in 1810, he became the head of the philosophy faculty and the university's rector.

Kant's impeccable scholarly reputation and formidable university stature – he had been dean of the philosophy faculty and the university's rector as well – did not protect him from the censors. His work *Religion within the Limits of Reason Alone* (1792) caught their attention and in 1794 Kant received a threatening letter from the king himself, Friedrich William, as represented by his minister of spiritual affairs and education Johann Christoph Wöllner (1732–1800), the substance of which is as follows:

> Our most high person has long observed with great displeasure how you misuse your philosophy to distort and disparage many of the cardinal and foundational teachings of the Holy Scriptures and of Christianity; how you have done this specifically in your

> book, 'Religion within the Limits of Reason Alone,' and similarly in other shorter treatises. We expected better of you, since you yourself must see how irresponsibly you have acted against your duty as a teacher of youth and against our sovereign purposes, of which you are well aware. We demand that you immediately give a conscientious vindication of your actions, and we expect that in the future, to avoid our highest disfavor, you will be guilty of no such fault, but rather, in keeping with your duty, apply your authority and your talents to the progressive realization of our sovereign purpose. Failing this, you must expect unpleasant measures for your continuing obstinacy.[4]

It was consequently forbidden to teach Kant's book. This is not altogether surprising, given how he subordinated the status of biblical revelation to the absolute authority of reason:

> universal human reason must be recognized and honored as supreme commanding principle in a natural religion within the Christian doctrine of faith; whereas the doctrine of revelation, upon which a church is founded and which stands in need of scholars as interpreters and preservers, must be cherished and cultivated as a mere means, though a most precious one, for giving meaning, diffusion, and continuity to natural religion even among the ignorant.[5]

Acquiescing to the king's dictate – reasonably enough since he was getting old and being threatened by the highest Prussian authority – Kant nonetheless defended himself with a thoughtfully detailed reply where he explained, first of all, that his classroom lectures had no religious content, and second, that his book was entirely consistent with acknowledging revelation as a way to understand the essence of Christianity and that in this, he did not disrespect Christianity in the least. When Friedrich William died in 1797, Kant considered himself released from the royal command and continued to publish on religious subjects, as in *The Conflict of the Faculties* (1798). At this point, though, he had retired from teaching the year before and was now 73, gradually losing his memory and having lost the sight in his left eye four years earlier due to a cataract.

In the year following Friedrich William's death Kant published his only textbook, *Anthropology from a Pragmatic Point of View* (1798). He was conscientious about the lectures on anthropology that he gave virtually every year from the early 1770s until his retirement two decades later – a subject he considered to be his own innovation and a practical accompaniment to the more abstract thoughts in his critical philosophy. As far as Kant's own view of his philosophical mission, self-conception and overall comprehension of his role and responsibilities as a university lecturer is concerned, his lectures on anthropology cannot be set aside as secondary, peripheral or as unimportant aspect of his philosophical oeuvre. They are a substantial accompaniment to his critical philosophy and his self-conception as a teacher, as is clear from how he described his overall philosophical vision:

> The plan I prescribed for myself a long time ago calls for an examination of the field of pure philosophy with a view to solving three problems: (1) What can I know? (metaphysics). (2) What ought I to do? (moral philosophy). (3) What may I hope? (philosophy of religion). A fourth question ought to follow, finally: What is man? (anthropology, a subject on which I have lectured for over twenty years).[6]

Given Kant's greatness and immeasurable influence as a philosopher, there has always been a temptation to underplay his lectures on anthropology and physical geography, along with some other works such as his *Observations on the Feeling of the Beautiful and the Sublime* (1764), for they contain some unforgettably off-putting remarks such as the following:

> Indeed, Father Labat reports that a Negro carpenter, whom he reproached for haughty treatment of his wives, replied: You whites are real fools, for first you concede so much to your wives, and then you complain when they drive you crazy.

There might be something here worth considering, except for the fact that this scoundrel was completely black from head to foot, a distinct proof that what he said was stupid.[7]

Humanity has its highest degree of perfection in the white race. The yellow Indians have a somewhat lesser talent. The Negroes are much lower, and lowest of all is part of the American races.[8]

Those having insight into something according to analogy by means of images, have a use of reason, but not from concepts. It seems that for a large part of the human race, nature has failed them with regard to the faculty of judging from concepts. All Oriental peoples belong to this part. From this it follows that with them the whole of morality cannot be pure, because it [morality] must be cognized from concepts. The pure moral concept is lacking in their morality, hence in their case nothing can arise from the principle of morality.[9]

Comments such as these have led some contemporary scholars to impugn Kant's moral character:

First and foremost, it is a 'nasty little secret' about Kant that, alongside his official cosmopolitan concern for all human beings (or, more accurately, and significantly differently, for the 'rationality' in all human beings), he harbored some very intellectually irresponsible (i.e. empirically counter evidenced, unevidenced, or at best underevidenced) and morally objectionable prejudices about human beings of various sorts. In particular, he was a misogynist, an antisemite (a passage in his Lectures on Ethics in effect says that all Jews are liars because all Jews are cowards), and a racist (he published a seminal essay on racial taxonomy, and makes wholesale negative remarks about such races as African negroes in his Anthropology).[10]

The above comment is from a respected scholar. As such, the accusations are of the kind that could be used with authority by those on a crusade to argue for the exclusion of Kant's writings from educational curricula and the removal of public memorials to him. A situation such as this calls for Kant's comments to be understood with closer attention to the details of the context.

As far as Kant's misogynism is concerned, it is there, but his attitude was an artefact of his times and Königsberg's conservative social environment. It is not as if Kant had nothing good to say about women. The fact, however, is that he lived in a 'society in which women start out on an unequal footing and then live out their lives that way, where women – especially women – must perpetually walk a tightrope between being treated as things and treated as persons'.[11]

With regard to Kant's alleged antisemitism, Kant was not an antisemite in his personal relationships. Clear evidence of this is his extreme fondness for Marcus Herz and Moses Mendelssohn, his professional support for Isaac Abraham Euchel and how he always kindly greeted Fanny Lewald's grandfather on his daily walks. Moreover, his critical attitude towards Judaism was not specific to that religion in some general respects. He maintained that its empirical content distracts people from apprehending the universal core of pure reason that underlies all religion – a criticism that he held in reference to Christianity and all other traditional religions, not to mention 'all Oriental peoples' as mentioned above.

As far as specific, contingent practices in the various traditional religions are concerned, Kant saw them all as pointing towards the same end, a universal rational religion that would eventually replace the individual traditional religions along with their arbitrarily grounded ritualistic practices and diversity of supposedly divine revelations – a religion of rational faith based exclusively and purely on the respect for morality that everyone has within themselves:

> Whether the devout individual makes his statutory visit at church or undertakes a pilgrimage to the sanctuaries in Loretto or Palestine; whether he takes his formulas of prayer to the

> heavenly authority with his lips, or by means of a prayer-wheel, like the Tibetan . . . or whatever the surrogate for the moral service of God might be, it is all the same and of equal worth. – Differences of external form here count equally for nothing but everything depends, rather, upon the acceptance or the forsaking of the one single principle of becoming well-pleasing to God – [upon] whether [we do it] through moral disposition alone.[12]

Rousseau expressed essentially the same view:

> I am told that a revelation was needed to teach men the way God wanted to be served. They present as proof the diversity of bizarre forms of worship which have been instituted, and do not see that this very diversity comes from the fancifulness of revelations. As soon as peoples took it into their heads make God speak, each made Him speak in its own way and made Him say what it wanted. If one had listened only what God says to the heart of man, there would never have been more than one religion on earth.[13]

With regard to the Jews as reported by his student Herder, Kant did refer publicly to how Judaic scriptures (allegedly) gave instructions about how to behave towards non-Jews, namely, as 'permitted by the Talmud to practice deceit'.[14] This was in the early 1760s, when Kant was in his late thirties. The above remark about cowardice is taken from the same early lectures on ethics that Herder recorded. This was before Kant read Rousseau and had developed a greater sense of personal humility. Three decades later, though, there remains an undercurrent of disapproval of the Jews as a group, albeit in a more tempered, qualified and more descriptive form, in a footnote from his 1790s anthropology textbook:

> The Palestinians [that is, Jews] living among us since their exile, or at least the great majority of them, have earned the not unfounded reputation of being cheaters, due to their spirit of usury. Admittedly it seems strange to think of a nation of

> cheaters; but it is just as strange to think of a nation of nothing but merchants, the far greater majority of whom are bound by an ancient superstition recognized by the state they live in, seek no civil honor, but rather wish to replace their loss through the advantage of outwitting the people under whom they find protection, and even one another. It cannot be otherwise with an entire nation of nothing but merchants, as non-productive members of society (for example, the Jews in Poland). So their constitution, which is sanctioned by ancient statutes and even by us under whom they live (who have certain holy books in common with them) cannot be repealed without inconsistency, even though they have made the saying 'Buyer beware' into the highest principle of their morality in dealing with us.[15]

As we know, Kant placed a premium on honesty. He found the supposed permission to lie stated in the Judaic scriptures to be morally intolerable and accordingly condemned the Jews as a group, probably in conjunction with an accurate perception of how closely adherent the Jews were to their holy scriptures. His position was based upon principle and what he believed were facts, rather than upon prejudice against this or that individual who had personally offended him in public, of which there are no accounts.

It is difficult to find passages in the Talmud to which Kant refers. Those that are often referred to as condoning lying to non-Jews are either fabricated, misquoted or refer to very specific situations, sometimes difficult to interpret, that resist generalization. So Kant does not appear to have had an informed understanding of the Talmud's religious directives. That he could have had a better understanding is unclear, although one can imagine that he might have brought up the subject, delicate as it was, with Moses Mendelssohn, who was familiar with the Torah and Talmud, before continuing to make public statements in his lectures.

Be that as it may, if one could find such passages in the 6,000-page long (in standard print) text of the Talmud – a task that amounts to looking for needles in a haystack – it would not follow that most Jews were aware of such passages as a matter of practical influence. Also, if such passages were indeed present and were made known, many reflective, morally conscious Jews might well have found them unacceptable, as did Kant, or perhaps outdated, understandable within the context of sixth-century Jewish society when the Talmud was written, but no longer.

Despite the above considerations, Kant did not have a positive opinion of Judaism as a religion. In the strict sense, he did not believe that in essence it was a religion at all, but more of a secular, political organization that appended an apparently moral component in the Ten Commandments – a set of rules that he understood as having been set out as authoritarian external directives in the absence of genuine moral motivation as he rationally understood it (whereas he believed that Christianity, through the sayings of Jesus, did display this kind of motivation). So it is not all that surprising that his various remarks about Judaism as a faith and Jews as a group lack a sympathetic tone. He wrote:

> The Jewish faith, as originally established, was only a collection of merely statutory laws supporting a political state; for whatever moral additions were appended to it, whether originally or only later, do not in any way belong to Judaism as such. Strictly speaking Judaism is not a religion at all but simply the union of a number of individuals who, since they belonged to a particular stock, established themselves into a community under purely political laws, hence not into a church; Judaism was rather meant to be a purely secular state, so that, were it to be dismembered through adverse accidents, it would still be left with the political faith (which pertains to it by essence) that this state would be restored to it (with the advent of the Messiah).[16]

Kant's racist remarks also deserve some reflection, because the label 'racist' without further explanation subjects him to a misunderstanding that confuses him with the majority of racists in our society, where racism is based on personal prejudice. But Kant had nothing to do with this style of thought and prejudice. His views were principled, if uninformed. For example, he read travel books and accounts of Asian religions, made judgements about the strong prevalence of imagistic mythology and concluded that those who originated the religions lacked the capacity for abstract thought – the kind of thought he believed was essential for genuine moral thinking. Without a developed capacity for abstract thought, it is impossible to formulate the categorical imperative and reflect upon whether the maxim of one's action can or cannot be generalized into a universal law.

So although it is undeniable that Kant had views that we would today call racist, he was an intellectual governed by reason almost exclusively in his opinions, rather than being a crude racist who irrationally condemns those of other groups due to perceived negative personal experiences with this or that individual or individuals of a different group. Referring to Kant as a racist without such qualification and understanding, as we see in the above quote from a contemporary scholar, invites misunderstanding, not to mention an uninformed and insufficiently justified condemnation of Kant as a person.

To further explain Kant's remarks about those of other races and religions, it helps to appreciate a more deep-rooted problem: Kant's Enlightenment style of thought itself invites the kinds of deprecating remarks of other groups that we find in his writings. This resides in the style's abstractive, generalizing, scientifically inspired disregard of details in an effort to seek the underlying principle, operative law or essence of the subject at hand. Such an approach works effectively in Newtonian physics, but it easily generates distortions when carried over into the anthropological context. Kant often speaks about other groups in the way tour books describe them: superficially and in caricature. In his book *Mythologies* (1957), the French literary theorist Roland Barthes (1915–1980) explains how unrealistic this style of thinking can be:

> For the Blue Guide [a book for tourists] exist only as 'types.' In Spain, for instance, the Basque is an adventurous sailor, the Levantine a light-hearted gardener, the Catalan a clever tradesman and the Cantabrian a sentimental highlander. We

> find again here this disease of thinking in essences, which is at the bottom of every bourgeois mythology of man (which is why we come across it so often). The ethnic reality of Spain is thus reduced to a vast classical ballet, a nice neat commedia dell'arte, whose improbable typology serves to mask the real spectacle of conditions, classes and professions.[17]

With the same awareness, Hegel condemned this style of superficial thinking in an essay entitled 'Who Thinks Abstractly?' (1808) where he wrote to similar effect: 'This is abstract thinking: to see nothing in the murderer except the abstract fact that he is a murderer, and to annul all other human essence in him with this simple quality.'[18] The idea is that when dealing with people, it is important to take into account each person as a concrete individual who fits a wide variety of categories, mother, daughter, niece, godmother, grandmother, neighbour, friend, colleague and so on, rather than to identify only one of these categories as the person's essence and to overlook the complex, multi-aspected reality of the person's being. Unfortunately, looking at people abstractively with a view towards formulating scientific-style generalizations leads to this kind of distortion.

So although we can find antisemitic and racist remarks in some of Kant's writings – they are not prevalent, but they are there – it is important to understand that Kant was not an antisemite or racist in the commonly understood hateful meaning of these words. Kant was a principled thinker in all of his beliefs and he treated everyone in his daily life with respect, no matter who they were. His antisemitic and racist comments boil down to his lack of information in conjunction with his commitment to abstractive thinking, scientific in inspiration and central to the style of his philosophizing, workable exceedingly well in certain areas of inquiry but not effectively in others.

With respect to condemning Kant as a racist or antisemite, there is the question of how much we can expect from a person. During Kant's time, there were indeed more insightful people in this regard. Kant uncritically adopted some of his questionable views from comments made by David Hume – a theorist for whom he generally had a great admiration – who in his essay 'Of Natural Characters' (1748) stated that darker-skinned people from Africa are naturally inferior to those who are white-skinned. Objecting to Hume's position, James Beattie (1735–1803), a Scottish poet and philosopher, said the following:

> That a negro-slave, who can neither read nor write, nor speak any European language, who is not permitted to do any thing but what his master commands, and who has not a single friend on the earth, but is universally considered and treated as if he were a species inferior to the human; – that such a creature should so distinguish himself among Europeans, as to be talked of through the world as a man of genius, is surely no reasonable expectation. To suppose him of an inferior species, because he does not thus distinguish himself, is just as rational, as to suppose any private European of an inferior species, because he has not raised himself to the condition of royalty.[19]

In sum, it helps to put Kant's racist and antisemitic remarks into perspective. His character was good and he developed his opinions based on principle. But he was uninformed. Perhaps with some extra reflection he might have shied away from some of his claims, since Beattie's critical comments on Hume show that even in the eighteenth century, it was possible to have a more realistic, humanly caring level of insight.

Most telling here, though, is that there are strong contemporary arguments in favour of the view that the standard or commonly held conception of race is itself without any validity.[20] That is, there is no such thing as 'race' in the following sense, which can be referred to specifically as a 'racialist' concept of race, defined as

> The familiar pernicious traditional, essentialist, and hierarchical race concept often mistakenly identified as the race concept. It maintains that races have intrinsic biological essences, are distinguished by normatively important features such as

intelligence and moral character, and can, on the basis of these features, be objectively ranked as superior and inferior.[21]

This racialist concept of race underlies Kant's comments and if indeed there is no reality to it, referring to Kant as a racist can be reduced to the matter of judging the basis of his attitudes – that is, attitudes he formed on the basis of principle rather than personal prejudice – rather than understanding him as referring objectively to any genuine truths about how people actually are.

In 1789, at age 65, Kant had already started to feel the effects of ageing, noting to one of his students that he was no longer able to study in the evenings, but needed to engage in lighter diversions to ensure a good night's sleep. He was soon only able to work for a couple of hours in the morning, after which time he would become drowsy. By 1795, a year before he retired from teaching, he noticed that his memory was starting to fail, as he sometimes forgot things or lost his train of thought. And this condition intensified to the point where his memory loss became increasingly apparent. When he reached age 74 in 1798, he was tired most of the time, with the bulk of his time devoted to eating, moving about and sleeping. With a strong will, he kept to his schedule as much as he could, continuing to visit the Motherby home on Sundays, but it was clear to everyone that he was losing his grip on things.

Kant's last couple of years were those of someone trying hard to maintain a failing mind and body. He wrote notes of his conversations so that he could remember their contents and was soon unable to write or answer letters. His body weakened to the point where he would sometimes fall down during his daily walks, fall off of his chair at home or fall asleep at the table, where his head would drop, letting his cap catch fire from the candles. He also began to suffer from nightmares – imagining that murderers were coming to kill him in his bed – and from what we call 'earworms' (stuck song syndrome), where songs kept playing repeatedly in his head unstoppably.[22]

Noticing that Kant was becoming infirm and unable to manage his affairs effectively, his long-time servant Martin Lampe – a person who developed drinking problems of his own – became lax in his duties to the point where Kant, himself not being able to function effectively, felt the need to dismiss Lampe in early 1802. At this point, Kant had not been out of his house for two years. Whether he knew that Lampe was stealing from him is unclear, but an unforgivable insult that came Kant's way sealed Lampe's fate.

After the dismissal, Kant dutifully maintained Lampe with a pension and wrote a letter of recommendation for him. A new servant was hired and during the last few months of Kant's life his remaining sister Katharina, the youngest of his sisters, compassionately helped her brother along with Wasianski, Kant's former student and pastor, who visited Kant frequently and recorded the details of Kant's final weeks and approach to the day when his life ended peacefully on 12 February 1804. As the concluding day came near, bedridden and unable to move, Kant beckoned with his lips to kiss his sister in thanks and thereafter, Wasianski as well, in a final, heartbreaking goodbye.

Visitors to Kant's house to pay their respects were surprised to see how thin and frail he had become, but his funeral was magnificent, fitting to his stature as one of history's most influential philosophers:

> On the 28th of February, at two o'clock in the afternoon, all the dignitaries of church and state, not only those resident in Konigsberg, but from the remotest parts of Prussia, assembled in the church of the castle. Hence they were escorted by the whole body of the university, splendidly dressed for the occasion, and by many military officers of rank, with whom Kant had always been a great favourite, to the house of the deceased professor; from which the corpse was carried by torchlight, the bells of every church in Konigsberg tolling, to the cathedral, which was lit up by innumerable wax-lights. A never-ending train of people followed it on foot. In the cathedral, after the usual burial rites, accompanied with every possible expression of national veneration to the deceased, there was a grand musical service, most admirably performed; at the close of which, Kant's mortal

Friedrich Bils, *Kant at His Lectern Reading a Book*, 19th century, lithograph.

remains were lowered into the academic vault; and there he now rests among the patriarchs of the university.[23]

As could be expected, a demand quickly arose for the purchase of 'Kant relics' after his death, such as his items of clothing and household items. His thirty-year-old sleeping cap, worthless in itself, sold for a high price. It was also customary at the time to purchase ringlets of the deceased's hair, about which his student Jachmann made the wry comment that 'like the relics of the saints, soon there will be more Kantian hair rings in the public than Kant had individual hairs in his whole life.'[24] Indeed, people's profit-seeking dispositions have not changed in some respects. A 1953 article in *ArtNews* echoed the same mentality in reference to the works of the French landscape painter Camille Corot (1796–1875), one of the most frequently forged painters in history: 'There is a saying in France that Corot painted two thousand canvases, five thousand of which are in America.'[25]

In his *Phenomenology of Spirit*, much in Kant's demythologizing manner, Hegel exposed the futility of the perennial attraction for obtaining and worshipping relics. We may be tempted to believe that something of a person's spirit, wisdom or good will resides in the person's bones, belongings or surroundings, mysteriously transferrable over to us, but this is a common illusion. If there is a desire to become closer to Mozart's musical genius, it will not help to touch the keys on Mozart's piano or own a locket of his hair (one sold at auction in 2015 for £35,000). Playing and studying his music is the proper path. If there is a desire to understand Kant, it is misguided to want to own his cap, visit his grave or get a close look at his death mask. One must read his books, which is where his thoughts and spirit reside.

Resting in peace was not quite the fate of Kant's body. Six years after Kant's initial burial, Kant's friend Johann Georg Scheffner (1736–1820) sponsored the construction of a small chapel area – the Stoa Kantiana – in the cathedral to which Kant's remains were transferred. The dedication ceremony took place around Easter 1810 and was attended by university professors, students and people from the community, as was appropriate for the occasion. After a lecture celebrating Kant, the group proceeded to the cathedral, where a pedestal was unveiled at the centre of the chapel, topped by the 1808 marble bust of Kant by Johann Gottfried Schadow (1764–1850), beneath which Kant's body was buried. Initially, the chapel was constructed in a modest style, but later images show, in obvious appreciation of Kant's philosophical stature, a large reproduction of Raphael's *School of Athens* (1509–11) on the wall behind Kant's bust, honouring him with a comparison to Plato and Aristotle.

With the passing of time, the chapel suffered significant neglect and Kant's body was exhumed for anatomical analysis seventy years

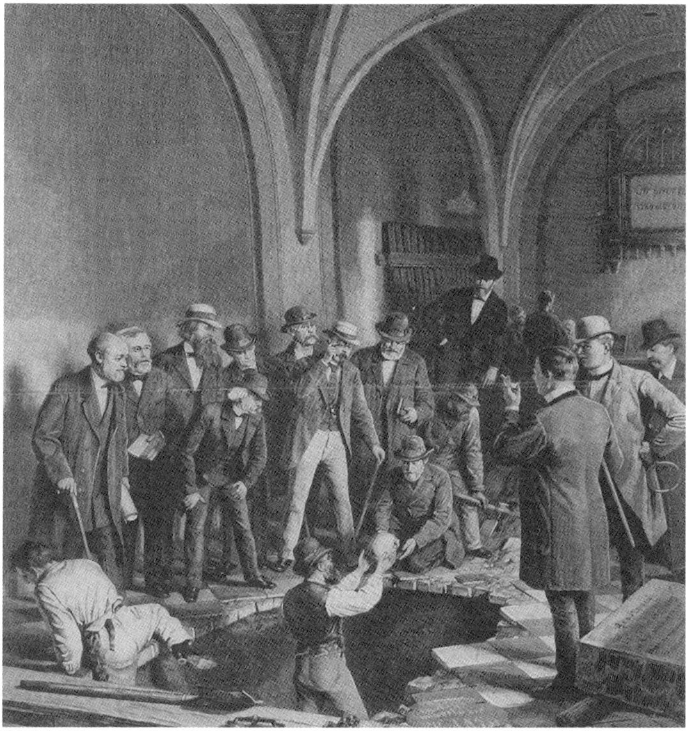

Exhumation of Kant's Remains, woodcut after chalk drawing by Johannes Heydeck, *c.* 1880.

later in 1880. The professors and administrators in charge of the digging uncovered a few skeletons in the cathedral floor, leading to some uncertainty about which body was Kant's. The deterioration of the coffins prevented a clear determination, but after they compared one of the skulls with the plaster cast of Kant's head that was made upon his death, the correct skeleton was identified. Aside from the skull's unusually large size – a size that the anatomists later attributed to extraordinarily developed parietal and occipital lobes – one of the key identifiers was the exact correspondence between the protruding lower lip on the plaster cast and a protruding lower canine tooth in the skull. Also worth noting is the striking

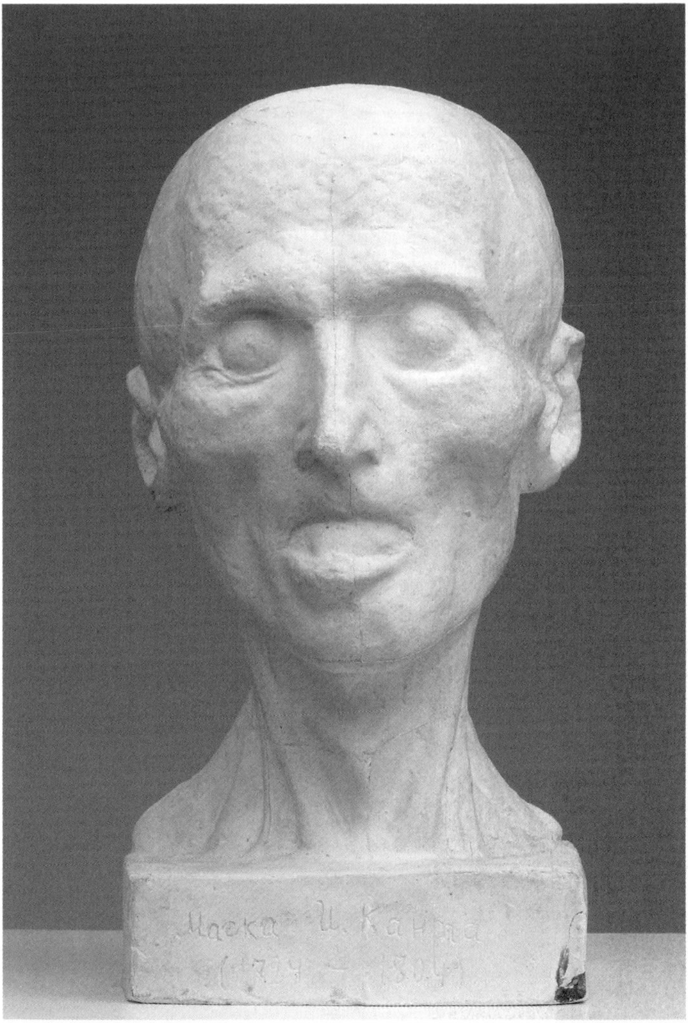

Andreas Knorre, Kant's death mask, 1804.

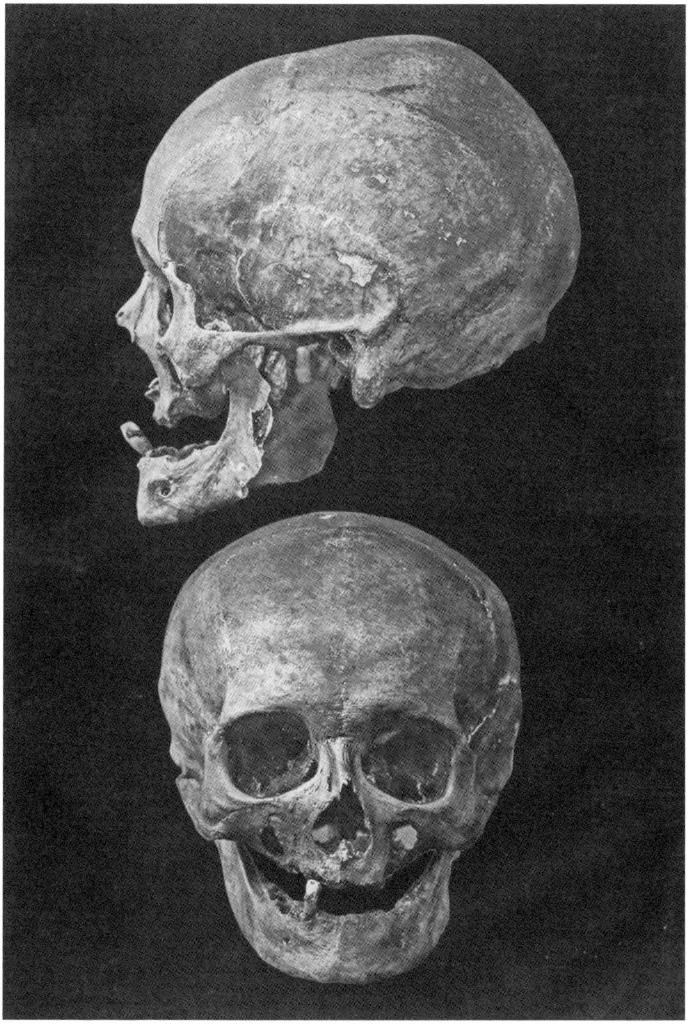

Kant's skull, photograph by Carl Kupffer and F. Bessel Hagen, 1881.

Kant's tomb.

congruency between photographs of Kant's skull and Karl Friedrich Hagemann's 1801 bust of Kant (illustrated earlier), which was done from life.

After the exhumation, Kant's body was moved yet again to the outside of the cathedral over which was erected a neo-Gothic chapel, where the body is said to rest. In 1924 – the bicentenary of Kant's birth – the chapel was replaced with a classical-style colonnade that presently surrounds the tomb. Remarkably, Kant's tomb survived the Second World War bombing that destroyed most of the cathedral, where it still stands today. Good fortune, however, does not always prevail. In his book *Kant* (1965), Uwe Schultz mentions that in 1950 Kant's tomb was broken into and that the body was stolen. The present-day tomb might very well be empty.[26]

Epilogue: Kant's Legacy

Entire books have been written on specific historical phases of Kant's influence, such as his impact on German university life during the later nineteenth century, so to review Kant's far-reaching intellectual impact would require volumes. To display the power of his ideas, we will look at only a segment of his most notable areas of influence in connection with philosophers and theorists of well-known international stature. For a sense, though, of a mere nineteen-year span of how the shape of German academics changed in view of Kant's thought, consider the following:

> From 1862 to 1881 the number of lecture courses on Kant trebled, and there were more lectures on Kant than all modern philosophers combined. Bibliographies show that, after 1860, the number of works on Kant increased geometrically every year. And, by 1870, every major German university had at least one neo-Kantian professor on its philosophy faculty, which was better representation than any other philosophical standpoint or tendency.[1]

Let us then consider Kant's influence on German Idealism and Marxism, Arthur Schopenhauer, Martin Heidegger, hermeneutics and a group that includes linguists and anthropologists who can be referred to as 'Linguo-Kantians'.

German Idealism and Marxism

As discussed earlier, central to Kant's theory of knowledge is the idea of the 'I', inspired by a tradition in philosophy initiated by Descartes in his *Meditations on First Philosophy* (1641) – a groundbreaking work wherein he describes himself famously as sitting before the fireplace one evening, wondering, with all of his philosophical energies, about that in which he can reliably believe. After a series of reflections, he concludes that even within the context of the most extremely deceptive forces, still, he cannot doubt that he exists, simply because he is aware of himself as immersed within that devilishly deceptive context. Hitting bedrock, he proclaims that whenever he says to himself, 'I think, I exist' or 'I think, therefore I am,' certainty has to prevail. From this foundation followed a style of modern philosophizing centred upon and extending from the subject of experience, the 'I', or, more precisely, immediate, self-conscious awareness.

As we have seen, this Cartesian 'I' emerges again in Kant's theory of knowledge, albeit in a highly generalized form, as the basis of all we can know about the world, where the long-term sense of always 'being me', abstractly considered, independently of any particular experiences, is regarded as that which holds together or *comprehends* not only the experiences of a lifetime, but the moment-to-moment apprehension of objects such as tables and chairs. The concept of an 'object in general' that this impersonal and abstracted 'I' projects, along with a set of subordinate logical categories and the forms of space and time, serves to organize into an array of understandable items the manifold sensations that come to us from without.

Subsequent to Kant, German Idealist philosophers such as Fichte, Schelling and Hegel discerned a more articulated structure to the self-aware 'I'. Taking a step beyond regarding the 'I' merely as a combinatory function upon given sensations, as did Kant, they realized that in an act of reflection wherein one says 'That is me' or 'I am that,' or even says to oneself 'I think,' that in addition to there being a subject ('I') that projects an object ('me'), there follows immediately an *identity* between the subject and object as a matter of self-realization.

The German Idealists appreciated that the structure of self-consciousness is consequently tripartite: upon saying to oneself 'That is me,' there is an initial position, an opposition that proceeds out of the position and a subsequent *reconciliation* between the position and the opposition – a subject–object fusion or blend. This subject–object blend or 'melting together' was a revelation, for a new logic emerged where this tripartite structure issuing from the analysis of the 'I think, I exist' was seen generally to be applicable for understanding a wide array of subject-matter, much of which does not concern a person's reflection or self-consciousness at all.

Hence was established the guiding principle of German Idealistic thought – dialectical logic (sometimes described with the terms 'thesis, antithesis and synthesis') that extended from Kant's theory of knowledge – most articulately and comprehensively realized in Hegel's grand system of philosophy, where all reality compares to a seed that develops dialectically into a young plant and then, through struggle, into a beautiful flower that becomes aware of itself as such. Assuming classically that the rational is the real and the real is the rational, Hegel interpreted human history, despite its wars, conflicts and resolutions, as slowly transforming into a condition of moral perfection. As we can now see, this recalls Kant's own vision of the future, except that Hegel envisaged it to be realized here on Earth rather than in a transcendent beyond whose reality is, at best, a matter of rational faith.

Insofar as dialectical logic is the fruit of the German Idealists' reflection on Kant's theory of knowledge and its grounding in self-consciousness, it is worth highlighting one of Hegel's celebrated analyses and its resonance in Karl Marx's thought as an indication of Kant's quiet influence upon the contemporary world. This is his discussion of the master–servant relationship in the *Phenomenology of Spirit* that inspired both Simone de Beauvoir (1908–1986), in her account of the asymmetrical social relationships between men and women as described in *The Second Sex* (1949), and Frantz Fanon (1925–1961), who referred to Hegel's master–servant analysis in his discussion of the asymmetrical social relationships involved in colonialism and slavery in *Black Skin, White Masks* (1952).

Hegel observes that when a master initially takes on a servant, the master has total control and the servant has none. But as the servant begins to work for the master, the servant acquires power that renders the master dependent upon the servant, for the servant learns how to manage important aspects of the master's life that the master does not have the interest or time to know about. Although the master always retains the upper hand and the servant never achieves equality, Hegel reveals that this dominance/submission condition in general is a no-win situation for each participant, for neither the master nor the servant obtains the recognition that is implicitly sought. The servant obtains recognition from the master, but disrespectfully, as an object to be used; the master obtains recognition from the servant, but by a relatively meaningless subordinate. In the end, both are frustrated: the servant feels objectified and the master feels empty. Hence derives the ultimately unsatisfying nature of dominance/submission relationships of

Frantz Fanon at a press conference in Tunis, 1959.

Simone de Beauvoir, 1952.

whatever kind. Only in a more balanced social world where people respect each other equally can such asymmetries be overcome.

In Marx, an asymmetrical, dominance/submission relationship of the above kind plays out at the social level between the capitalist masters and the worker servants, and within this context he accordingly envisions a development that dissolves the asymmetry, at least in principle. The capitalist private property owners employ workers as wage labourers to make products for them to sell. They own the wage labourers, in effect, as their servants. They also pay the workers as little as possible – pure subsistence, ideally – and sell the products of the workers' labour, which they own, for the highest price possible to accumulate profits for themselves.

In this arrangement – admittedly extremely simplified in the present description – the expectation is the following. First, the capitalists grow richer and the workers grow poorer. As the capitalists compete with each other, their numbers are reduced, concentrating the available money into fewer hands. As the number of workers becomes conspicuously greater than that of the capitalists and as the workers become self-aware of this unjust disproportion and their implicit as-yet untapped power, the possibility of a workers' revolution surfaces into social consciousness. As the workers' impoverishment reaches a point of desperation, the pressure leads to an overthrow of the capitalists where the workers assume control of the factories and natural resources to become *worker/owners*, socially together as one and equal in status.

On this model, idealized as it is (for the capitalists have many ways to prevent their overthrow), the opposition between 'capitalist master' and 'worker servant' is reconciled, blended and dissolved through social revolution in the dialectical logical style of opposition and reconciliation. Insofar as Marx's visionary ideas have influenced a large part of the world and insofar as their dialectical basis can be traced back through German Idealism into Kant's theory of knowledge, there is a virtually unappreciated presence of Kant's philosophizing in the history of Marxism.

Arthur Schopenhauer (1788–1860)

When he began his university studies in philosophy, Schopenhauer first studied Plato and Kant, both of whom captured his imagination. Most impressive was their shared view that the ordinary world in which we live is not ultimately real. Schopenhauer expressed this by saying that life is a 'dream' or 'phantasmagoria', echoing Plato's view that our spatio-temporal world is a world of 'becoming', never completely true, and Kant's view that the world is merely an appearance of an unknowable 'thing in itself'. Schopenhauer asserted further that life is 'suffering', which provides some insight into how he understood the basic condition of our daily lives. In this regard, referring to the world as a 'nightmare' would be more apt.

Similar to Herder's dedicated attendance and documenting of Kant's lectures, Schopenhauer attended Fichte's lectures as a university student, studying his ideas carefully and taking extensive, almost book-length notes. Although he eventually became disillusioned with Fichte's philosophy, he adopted a central idea that Fichte inherited from Kant: that our will is the most significant aspect of our being, for them understood morally as an expression of our freedom.

Schopenhauer always professed that he was a Kantian who simply developed the implications of what Kant wrote. Fichte conceived of his relation to Kant in the same way. How Schopenhauer did this, though, lent an unexpected twist to the reason-based, moral conception of will that Kant and Fichte advocated, for Schopenhauer regarded the will in a radically different manner as a non-rational, non-moral, essentially meaningless, blind urge that resides at the basis of every living thing and of reality as a whole. Despite this alternative conception, it precipitated a vision of the human condition akin to Kant's, insofar as Kant had a dim view of the standing human condition, with selfishness and violence as all-too-prevalent and permeating.

With his new conception of the world as 'will', Schopenhauer was able to explain more directly *why* the world is filled with selfishness, suffering and violence. It resides in the very nature of reality: we, and everything else, are constituted by a blind, driving energy – 'will', the ultimate core of all that is – that when it individuates and objectifies into the realm of space and time generates a world theatre of self-serving individuals, each set on survival and each competing with the others in a 'war of all against all', as Thomas Hobbes described the animalistic state of nature. As constituted by 'will', every person is filled with desire – indeed, with so many desires that it is impossible to satisfy them all, turning life into a realm of unremitting frustration. Agreeing with the Buddhist view that desire causes suffering – a religion with which Schopenhauer closely identified – Schopenhauer recognized a need for enlightenment and relief from the vicious dog-eat-dog, spatio-temporal world.

Consistent with the fire-and-brimstone Christian vision where everyone is a priori considered to be a sinner in need of redemption, not to mention the more specific Pietist tradition that says the same, Schopenhauer outlined paths to enlightenment, each of which involves the minimization of our sense of individuality as a being in space and time, and hence a minimization of the multitude of desires that constantly press upon us. The first is the experience of beauty, where we contemplate the perfected form of a beautiful object and experience a feeling of transcendence, similar to how Plato described the apprehension of the absolute form of beauty as lifting us out of the ordinary spatio-temporal world. The second is the experience of morality, where, similar to Kant, we realize that each of us is constituted by the same timeless, universal substance, one and the same inner being, and that when someone else feels pain, there is a real sense in which it is our own pain. John Donne expressed the idea in his famous meditation from 1624:

> No man is an Iland, intire of it selfe; every man is a peece of the Continent, a part of the maine; if a Clod bee washed away by the Sea, Europe is the lesse, as well as if a Promontorie were, as well as if a Mannor of thy friends or of thine owne were; any mans death diminishes me, because I am involved in Mankinde;
> And therefore never send to know for whom the bell tolls;
> It tolls for thee.[2]

For Schopenhauer, the universal commonality expressed in our moral awareness is not our dispassionate rationality, as it is for Kant, but the feeling of compassion, which resonates with the main principle of Buddhist ethics. His differences with Kant regarding the basis of morality notwithstanding, Schopenhauer shares Kant's view that morality and universality go together, contrary to the forces of individuality and selfishness.

As the final step to enlightenment, Schopenhauer advocated an extreme minimization of desire in an ascetic lifestyle, governed by what he called the attitude of 'denial' of one's will. The upshot is a supreme sense of liberation from the pressures of desire, like the relief from a major addiction, closely akin to how Buddhists describe enlightenment as the relief from worldly desire and the frustrating grasping for objects that are inherently impermanent. The leading

Ludwig Sigismund Ruhl, *Arthur Schopenhauer*, *c.* 1815, oil on canvas.

ideas in both are 'liberation', 'release' and the realization that desires are essentially empty and void.

As a philosopher who substantially absorbed Kant's philosophy, Schopenhauer was himself extremely influential, especially in literature and the arts, where his theory of music was taken up by the composer Richard Wagner (1813–1883), who fundamentally changed the course of Western music. Others whom Schopenhauer influenced include Friedrich Nietzsche as well as great literary figures such as Samuel Beckett, Jorge Luis Borges, Joseph Conrad, André Gide, Thomas Hardy, D. H. Lawrence, Thomas Mann, Guy de Maupassant, Herman Melville, Edgar Allan Poe, Leo Tolstoy and Emile Zola. Via Schopenhauer's influence, all of these creative minds can be said to have been working in Kant's shadow.

Martin Heidegger (1889–1976), Hermeneutics and the Linguo-Kantians

The discipline of hermeneutics or theory of interpretation has its roots in the interpretation of the Bible, where readers are faced with the task of interpreting God's word (which is how the Bible's authorship has been understood by many) in its originally intended meaning. For the general public, this was at first not especially problematic, given a prevailing faithful reliance upon the members of the priesthood to transmit the true meaning of God's message. With the Protestant Reformation, however, which Karl Marx so aptly described as Martin Luther's having 'transformed the priests into laymen by turning laymen into priests',[3] interpretation of the Bible became legitimately open to everyone, which added debate and uncertainty about how exactly one should interpret God's words, either literally or metaphorically, for example. Hence arose the many different branches of Protestantism.

In legal contexts as well, as questions persisted about how one should interpret the many volumes of written laws, there soon arose a need for a general theory of interpretation applicable not only to religious and legal texts, but to all texts and linguistic utterances. Hermeneutics accordingly developed into a discipline whose aim is to understand the dynamics of our most basic level of communication that involves not only linguistic expressions, but artistic expressions and behaviours such as gestures and facial expressions. Although usually not appreciated as such, hermeneutics as the study of how we discern meaning is among the most fundamental disciplines of all.

The German theologian and philosopher Friedrich Schleiermacher (1768–1834) is recognized as among the first theorists to develop a general theory of interpretation, often quoted as saying that our task as interpreters is to understand an author better than he understood himself. For Schleiermacher, this involves considering a text's objective grammatical structures as expressions of the author's specifically intended meaning, the reproduction and grasping of which is the ultimate aim of interpretation, that is, replicating to ourselves the author's intention, truly becoming one with what the author had in mind.

As it turns out, the more one reflects upon how the process of interpretation should proceed, the more complicated and convoluted it becomes. Words have many meanings; the internal states of people's minds are essentially inscrutable, sometimes to the authors themselves; texts have a multiplicity of aspects with a seemingly endless linguistic resonance and train of associations; and, on top of this, attention to this or that aspect can be highlighted or set into the background when constructing a theory of interpretation.

Some generations after Schleiermacher, a theorist who was sensitive to these nuances and complications in the act of interpretation and who developed a theory of interpretation after having studied Schleiermacher's work carefully was Wilhelm Dilthey (1833–1911), a German philosopher, historian, sociologist and psychologist. There is no need here to describe Dilthey's complex account of interpretation, except to mention that, consistent with Kant's lifelong view that natural science is unable to understand the nature of life, Dilthey maintained that there is a difference between the natural sciences and the humanistic and social sciences, and that understanding or interpreting the significance of the latter requires a different interpretive method from using pure mathematics. Second, rather than attending to the individual author and grammar too narrowly as relatively isolated and focused objects of interpretation, Dilthey broadened the interpretative framework to include a consideration of the historical context of the author and the texts that we are trying to understand. Those who live in different historical periods can have significantly different styles of thought and these need to be taken into account when trying to understand the expressions from any particular time period.

Inspired by Dilthey's historical emphasis, Martin Heidegger more reflectively drew attention to the importance of recognizing the interpreter's own historical situatedness in the process of interpretation. Thinking further about the condition of the *interpreter* rather than of the objects of interpretation, he realized that as a historically situated person, every interpreter approaches every object of interpretation with a set of expectations and projections of possible meaning that derive from their past experience and concrete situation. As he says, every act of interpretation is 'always done under the guidance of a point of view, which fixes that with regard to which what is understood is to be interpreted', and that 'an interpretation is never a presuppositionless apprehending of something presented to us.'[4]

The insight is directly from Kant, whose theory of knowledge develops the idea that the mind is not blank or presuppositionless to begin with, as the British empiricists assumed, but has a structure that it brings to experience and that actively constitutes our perception of the world. Within the hermeneutical context, instead of speaking of space, time and the categories of the understanding as did Kant, we bring to experience a set of expectations that have been unreflectively absorbed from our given situation in the world. From the very start, these determine how we comprehend the object to be interpreted. One could call them 'prejudgements' that initially guide our interpretation, as did Hans-Georg Gadamer (1900–2002), a philosopher who cultivated Heidegger's hermeneutical views in his book *Truth and Method* (1975).

Martin Heidegger, *c.* 1927.

To appreciate this Kantian influence in hermeneutics, consider a situation where it would be possible to hear exactly the same sonic impressions as did the audience who listened to an early performance of one of Beethoven's symphonies – one conducted by Beethoven himself. Despite the sonic coincidence, it would remain impossible to hear the same music or interpret it in an identical fashion to those who lived centuries before. We have no choice but to hear the music with twenty-first-century ears, knowing the sounds of jazz, pop and later classical music, all of which unreflectively structure our expectations and understanding.

Similarly, imagine a theatre company that sought to perform one of Shakespeare's plays in the most authentic manner, replicating the accents and clothing, and doing its best to employ everything that could be learned to enable the audience to experience the play as it was originally presented. It would be no surprise to discover that as an oversight, the costumes were reconstructed noticeably with shiny plastic buttons, or that over the years some words have acquired resonances of meaning that would now make us laugh, but not any Elizabethan. It is not possible to set one's own historical situation and knowledge aside entirely, as if one were a disembodied, ahistorical, uninvolved interpreter, like an ideal scientific observer. In the act of interpretation, one is always involved and constitutively influential.

As a final example, consider someone who is committed to understanding the meanings of Plato's or Aristotle's ancient Greek texts and who spends years studying what we know of the ancient Greek language. Such conscientious efforts notwithstanding, the person inevitably must learn ancient Greek through a contemporary natural language that itself carries a set of valuations and ways of dividing the world, all of which enter into the learning and understanding of the ancient language, precluding the possibility of comprehending the language exactly as either Plato or Aristotle did.

The original meaning of the author or text may exist in principle as a fact to be discovered, but unveiling or revealing this meaning as it is in itself can never be achieved. Less extreme than Kant's view that knowledge of the thing-in-itself is impossible, our relationship to the author's or text's original meaning is more accurately described as translucent rather than opaque. We can approach the original meaning from various interpretive directions, but we will never apprehend it without having our own presuppositions and prejudgements infuse themselves into our understanding. By acknowledging our inescapable presence and contributing impact in the act of interpretation, we implicitly acknowledge, in one of the most fundamental academic disciplines, that Kant's influence powerfully endures more than two hundred years after his death.

Echoing these hermeneutical considerations, a similar Kantian influence obtained in the field of linguistics and anthropology. Consider this remarkably Kantian quote from the American linguist Benjamin Lee Whorf (1897–1941), written in 1940:

> We dissect nature along lines laid down by own native languages. The categories and types that we isolate from the world of phenomena we do not find there because they stare every observer in the face; on the contrary, the world is presented in a kaleidoscopic flux of impressions which has to be organized by our minds – and this means largely by the linguistic systems in our minds. We cut nature up, organize it into concepts, and ascribe significances as we do, largely because we are parties to an agreement to organize it in this way – an agreement that holds throughout our speech community and is codified in the patterns of our language. The agreement is, of course, an implicit and unstated one, but its terms are absolutely obligatory; we cannot talk at all except by subscribing to the organization and classification of data which the agreement decrees.[5]

Whorf describes the activity of natural languages in close parallel to how Kant describes the activities of space, time and the categories of the understanding: as organizing a 'kaleidoscopic flux of impressions' – what Kant would refer to as the 'manifold of sensation' – into the world of tables, chairs, trees and mountains in which we live and with which we are ordinarily familiar. Just as our minds are constructed unavoidably in a determinate way according to Kant, comparable to the prismatic structure of a fly's eye that the fly cannot remove, one's natural language along with the organizational structure it imposes on the world must be assumed if we want to talk to each other. Here, a given natural language assumes a role comparable to how space, time and the categories of the understanding operate in Kant's theory.

The crucial difference is that there are many different natural languages and hence many different ways of organizing the perceptual world, sometimes with striking differences between them. To describe time, for example, some languages such as English use three words – 'past', 'present' and 'future' – whereas others such as Hopi use only two: one word that refers to present and past together without any sharp distinction and another word that refers to what has not yet happened. Another example is languages that tend to conceive of daily objects as static things in contrast to others that tend to conceive of them as processes. Consider the human body or the body of any living being. The body can be referred to as a static thing that can be photographed or weighed upon a scale, but it can also be thought of as a continuously moving, swirling field of energetic particles, like a whirlpool that disappears once the water stops moving.

Although it is possible to appreciate in principle the differences between natural languages as just described, it might not be possible, or not easily possible, for people speaking one natural language to have the experiences of those who speak another when the respective ways in which each language comprehends the world is radically different. Whorf goes far in the latter direction, suggesting that there is a sense in which people with very different natural languages can live in different experiential worlds.

There is plenty of room for debate here and Whorf's view – inspired by his teacher and anthropologist Edward Sapir (1884–1939) – raises the issue of the *degrees* of similarity and difference that obtain between natural languages. At the other end of the spectrum from Whorf and Sapir, one can argue from the views of the linguist Noam Chomsky (1928–), in a manner even closer to Kant, that there is a common, universal basis for all natural languages and that the differences between them are less socially divisive than has been imagined. Such debates will go on, but we see here the continual presence of how Kantian ideas have entered into more recent developments concerning the nature of language and its impact on how we comprehend the world around us.

Heinrich Wolff, *Kant at his desk at home in his study*, 1909, lithograph.

An important development that follows from the substitution of natural languages for the traditional Kantian structures of the understanding is the opportunity for affecting social change. Suppose there is a gendered language where most of the words referring to higher political offices are male gendered, as is true in French, or a language where there is a complex hierarchy of addresses, where social statuses are distinctively layered in the grammatical structures, as in Thai. For those who are brought up in such natural languages, implicit messages and subtexts are communicated, such as the kind of people who are expected to hold high office, or the expected way to organize one's social relationships.

Of contemporary relevance is that the subtexts and implicit messages that natural languages carry can be brought into explicit consciousness and in some cases modified by changing the language, either in a liberating or oppressive way. To liberate, for example, one can modify sexist words that occur in a natural language. To oppress, a government can censor certain words to prevent the expression of truth. Either way, it is stunning to see how Kant's influence has extended centuries after his death, having so substantially permeated the contemporary fields of linguistics, anthropology, feminism and politics.

The theorists whose views we have briefly highlighted here – Hegel, Marx, Schopenhauer, Heidegger, Fanon, Beauvoir, Sapir, Whorf, Chomsky – are at the tip of the massive iceberg that represents Kant's legacy. We can imagine his influence as the ripples that extend from a raindrop that falls upon a quiet pond at the beginning of a cloudburst. And as the wind changes the storm-cloud patterns themselves, so have followed the transformations of Kant's ideas in their impact upon generation after generation of readers, still poised to inform a presently unwritten future.

References

Introduction

1 Heinrich Heine, 'On the History of Religion and Philosophy in Germany', in *On the History of Religion and Philosophy in German and Other Writings*, ed. Terry Pinkard and trans. Howard Pollack-Milgate (Cambridge, 2007), p. 79.
2 Arthur Schopenhauer, *The World as Will and Representation*, vol. II, trans. and ed. Judith Norman, Alistair Welchman and Christopher Janaway (Cambridge, 2018), p. 153.

2 Pietism, Kant, Königsberg and Casanova

1 August Hermann Francke, *Die siebente Predigt über das siebente Gebot, Schriften und Predigten*, vol. X: *Predigten* II, ed. Erhard Peschke. *Texte zur Geschichte des Pietismus* II.10. (Berlin, 2011), p. 406, trans. in Peter James Yoder, *Pietism and the Sacraments: The Life and Theology of August Hermann Francke* (University Park, PA, 2021), p. 52.
2 Quoted in Friedrich Paulsen, *Immanuel Kant: His Life and Doctrine*, trans. J. E. Creighton and Albert Lefevre (London, 1902), pp. 28–9, originally from the text of one of Kant's students and friends, Friedrich Theodor Rink, *Ansichten aus Immanuel Kant's Leben* (Königsberg, 1805), pp. 14–15, translation slightly modified.
3 Entries in the Collegium Fridericianum school records show Kant's surname is spelled variously as 'Cant', 'Cante', 'Kant', 'Kandt' and 'Candt'. Dr Rudolph Reike, ed., *Kantiana. Beiträge zu Immanuel Kants Leben und Schriften* (Königsberg, 1860), pp. 46–7.

4 Immanuel Kant, 'Anthropology from a Pragmatic Point of View', trans. Robert B. Louden, in *Immanuel Kant, Anthropology, History, and Education*, ed. Günter Zöller and Robert B. Louden (Cambridge, 2007), p. 232.

3 Kant at the University: The Living Body in a Mechanistic World

1 Immanuel Kant, *Thoughts on the True Estimation of Living Forces and Assessment of the Demonstrations that Leibniz and Other Scholars of Mechanics have made use of in this Controversial Subject, Together with Some Prefatory Considerations Pertaining to the Force of Bodies in General*, trans. Jeffrey B. Edwards and Martin Schönfeld, in *Immanuel Kant: Natural Science*, ed. Eric Watkins, trans. Lewis White Beck et al. (Cambridge, 2012), p. 125.

2 Ibid., p. 40.

3 Immanuel Kant, *Critique of the Power of Judgment*, ed. Paul Guyer, trans. Paul Guyer and Eric Matthews (Cambridge, 2000), p. 271.

4 Johann Georg Hamann, 'Two Dedications', from *Socratic Memorabilia* (1759), in *Johann Georg Hamann: Writings on Philosophy and Language*, trans. Kenneth Haynes (Cambridge, 2007), p. 6.

4 The Theist, Astronomer and Socialite

1 Immanuel Kant, *Correspondence*, ed. and trans. Arnulf Zweig (Cambridge, 1999), p. 56.

2 Immanuel Kant, 'The Only Possible Argument in Support of a Demonstration of the Existence of God [1763]', in *Immanuel Kant: Theoretical Philosophy, 1755–1770*, ed. and trans. David Walford and Ralf Meerbote (Cambridge, 1992), p. 111.

3 Ibid.

4 Immanuel Kant, *Observations on the Feeling of the Beautiful and Sublime and Other Writings*, ed. Patrick Frierson and Paul Guyer (Cambridge, 2011), pp. 58, 143, translation slightly modified.

5 Ibid., pp. 174, 22, translation slightly modified.

6 Ibid., p. 200.

5 The Best Friend, the Spirit-Seer and the Dogmatic Slumbers

1 Reinhold Bernhard Jachmann, *Immanuel Kant geschildert in Briefen einen Freund* (Königsberg, 1804), p. 77.
2 Immanuel Kant, *Observations on the Feeling of the Beautiful and Sublime and Other Writings*, ed. Patrick Frierson and Paul Guyer (Cambridge, 2011), p. 96.
3 Jean-Jacques Rousseau, *Emile; or, On Education*, trans. Allan Bloom (New York, 1979), p. 95.

6 The 'Silent Decade': Space and Time as 'Imaginary'

1 Ludwig Ernst Borowski, *Ueber Immanuel Kant, Darstellung des Lebens und Charakters Immanuel Kants* (Königsberg, 1804), p. 68.
2 Immanuel Kant, 'Anthropology Friedländer (1775–1776)', trans. G. Felicitas Munzel, in *Immanuel Kant: Lectures on Anthropology*, ed. Allen W. Wood and Robert B. Louden (Cambridge, 2012), pp. 205–6. Translation slightly modified. In a lecture a decade later Kant repeated the Heidegger story and said that when the clothes were switched, 'Heidegger looked like a witch. But she looked like a quite handsome male' (Immanuel Kant, 'Anthropology Mrongovius (1784–1785)', trans. Robert R. Clewis, p. 436 in the same volume mentioned above. In his *Anthropology from a Pragmatic Point of View* (1798), Kant repeated the same story.
3 Immanuel Kant, 'Essays Regarding the Philanthropinum [1776/1777]', trans. Robert B. Louden, in *Immanuel Kant: Anthropology, History, and Education*, ed. Günter Zöller and Robert B. Louden (Cambridge, 2007), p. 98.
4 Immanuel Kant, 'On the Form and Principles of the Sensible and the Intelligible World', in Immanuel Kant, *Theoretical Philosophy, 1755–1770*, trans. and ed. David Walford and Ralf Meerbote (Cambridge, 1992), p. 387.
5 Huineng, *The Sixth Patriarch's Dharma Jewel Platform Sutra*, trans. Buddhist Text Translation Society (Burlingame, CA, 2001), p. 109.
6 Immanuel Kant, *Correspondence*, ed. and trans. Arnulf Zweig (Cambridge, 1999), pp. 162–3.
7 Ibid., p. 163.
8 Ibid., p. 162.
9 Fanny Lewald, *Meine Lebensgeschichte* (Berlin, 1861), pp. 9–10. My translation.

10 Karl Abraham Freiherr von Zedlitz, 'Letter of August 1, 1778', quoted in Willibald Klinke, *Kant for Everyman*, trans. Michael Bullock (London, 1951), p. 31.

11 Immanuel Kant, 'The Conflict of the Faculties', trans. Mary J. Gregor and Robert Anchor, in *Immanuel Kant: Religion and Rational Theology*, trans. Allen Wood and George di Giovanni (Cambridge, 1996), p. 273.

12 Friedrich Nietzsche, *Beyond Good and Evil*, trans. Walter Kaufmann (New York, 1966), p. 206.

13 Immanuel Kant, *The Conflict of the Faculties*, trans. Mary J. Gregor (New York, 1979), p. 95. Note that feelings such as pity 'may' find their place, but need not.

7 Kant's 'Table Society' and His Battles against a New Era

1 Immanuel Kant, *Critique of the Power of Judgment*, ed. Paul Guyer, trans. Paul Guyer and Eric Matthews (Cambridge, 2000), p. 207n.

2 Immanuel Kant, 'Anthropology from a Pragmatic Point of View', trans. Robert B. Louden, in *Immanuel Kant: Anthropology, History, and Education*, ed. Günter Zöller and Robert B. Louden (Cambridge, 2007), pp. 380–81.

3 Immanuel Kant, 'Metaphysics of Morals', in *Immanuel Kant: Practical Philosophy*, trans. Mary J. Gregor (Cambridge, 1996), p. 551.

4 Immanuel Kant, 'Groundwork of the Metaphysics of Morals', in *Practical Philosophy*, trans. Gregor, p. 79.

5 Kant, 'Metaphysics of Morals', pp. 429–30.

6 Michel Foucault, *Discipline and Punish: The Birth of the Prison*, trans. Alan Sheridan (New York, 1977), p. 135.

7 Immanuel Kant, *Correspondence*, ed. and trans. Arnulf Zweig (Cambridge, 1999), p. 508.

8 *Vossische Zeitung*, 14 July 1776, in Robert Wendelin Keyserlingk, *Across Many Oceans: A Family Saga* (Montreal, 1984), p. 90.

9 G.W.F. Hegel, 'On the Positivity of the Christian Religion', in *Hegel: Early Theological Writings*, trans. T. M. Knox (Philadelphia, PA, 1948), pp. 169–70.

10 Immanuel Kant, 'Review of J. G. Herder's *Ideas for the Philosophy of the History of Humanity*. Parts 1 and 2', trans. Alan W. Wood, in *Anthropology, History, and Education*, ed. Zöller and Louden, p. 132.

11 Lewis White Beck, 'Sketch of Kant's Life and Work', in Immanuel Kant, *On History*, trans. Lewis White Beck (Indianapolis, IN, 1963), p. xxvii.

12 Reinhold Bernhard Jachmann, *Immanuel Kant geschildert in Briefen an einen Freund*, in *Immanuel Kant – Ein Lebensbild nach Darstellen der Zeitgenossen – Borowski, Jachmann, Wasianski*, ed. Hermann Schwarz (Halle, 1907), quoted and trans. Steve Naragon in '"A Good Honest Watchmaker": J.C.F. Schulz's Portrait of Kant from 1791', *Kant-Studien*, CI/2 (2010), p. 219.

13 Friedrich Schiller, 'On Grace and Dignity', in *Schiller's 'On Grace and Dignity' in Its Cultural Context: Essays and a New Translation*, ed. J. V. Curran and C. Fricker (Rochester, NY, 2005), p. 153.

8 The Writings of the 1780s: Kant's Three *Critiques*

1 Galileo Galilei, 'The Assayer', in *Discoveries and Opinions of Galileo*, trans. Simon Drake (New York, 1957), pp. 274 and 277.

2 Immanuel Kant, *Critique of Pure Reason*, trans. Paul Guyer and Allen W. Wood (Cambridge, 1998), pp. 159–60 (A26/B42; A27/B43).

3 Ibid., p. 117 (Bxxx). Kant's exact words are 'Ich mußte also das Wissen aufheben, um zum Glauben Platz zu bekommen', where in reference to 'knowledge', *aufheben* means more comprehensively that, as typically translated, he *restricted* knowledge to empirical knowledge, denying metaphysical knowledge, but that he also *preserved* the idea that empirical knowledge is powerful enough to yield natural laws in the face of Humean scepticism, as well as *enhanced* or 'lifted up' the idea of empirical knowledge by explaining its subjective sources in the *a priori* forms of space, time and the categories of the understanding. The word *aufheben* does not simply mean 'deny', 'cancel' or 'limit', but has a more complex threefold meaning: to cancel, preserve and enhance, all at once.

4 Immanuel Kant, 'Prolegomena to Any Future Metaphysics that Will Be Able to Come Forward as Science', trans. Gary Hatfield, in *Immanuel Kant: Theoretical Philosophy after 1781*, ed. Henry Allison and Peter Heath (Cambridge, 2002), p. 169.

5 Immanuel Kant, 'Critique of Practical Reason', trans. Mary Gregor, in *Immanuel Kant: Practical Philosophy*, trans. and ed. Mary Gregor (Cambridge, 1996), pp. 264–5.

6 'Aurelius Victor says that many men in the transports of love voluntarily bought a night with Cleopatra with their lives; and this sacrifice is not impossible for the drunkenness of passion. But let us suppose that the most desperate man – the one least in command

of his senses – sees the apparatus of torture and is sure of perishing on it in torments a quarter of an hour later. Not only would this man instantaneously become superior to temptations; it would even cost him little to resist them.' (Jean-Jacques Rousseau, *Emile; or, On Education*, trans. Allan Bloom (New York, 1979), p. 325).

7 Kant, 'Critique of Practical Reason', pp. 163–4.

8 Plato, 'The Apology' in *The Dialogues of Plato*, vol. II, trans. B. Jowett (Oxford, 1892), pp. 125–6.

9 Kant, 'Critique of Practical Reason', p. 244.

10 Ibid., p. 269.

11 Immanuel Kant, 'Religion within the Boundaries of Mere Reason', trans. George di Giovanni, in *Immanuel Kant: Religion and Natural Theology*, trans. and ed. Allen Wood and George di Giovanni (Cambridge, 1996), p. 93.

12 Immanuel Kant, *Critique of the Power of Judgment*, ed. Paul Guyer, trans. Paul Guyer and Eric Matthews (Cambridge, 2000), §84n, p. 301.

13 David Hume, 'Of the Standard of Taste', in *David Hume: Essays, Moral, Political, and Literary*, ed. Eugene F. Miller (Indianapolis, IN, 1985), pp. 234–5.

14 Kant, *Critique of the Power of Judgment*, §28, p. 144.

15 Ibid., §75, pp. 270–71.

16 Ibid., §17, p. 117; §82, pp. 294–5.

17 Ibid., §86, pp. 308–9 (translation slightly modified).

9 The Final Years

1 Immanuel Kant, *Correspondence*, ed. and trans. Arnulf Zweig (Cambridge, 1999), pp. 362–3.

2 Ibid., p. 559.

3 J. G. Fichte, 'On the Ground of Our Belief in a Divine World-Governance', in *J. G. Fichte and the Atheism Dispute (1798–1800)*, ed. Yolanda Estes and Curtis Bowman (Farnham, 2010), pp. 25–6.

4 Kant, *Correspondence*, p. 485.

5 Kant, 'Religion within the Boundaries of Mere Reason', trans. George di Giovanni, in *Immanuel Kant: Religion and Natural Theology*, trans. and ed. Allen Wood and George di Giovanni (Cambridge, 1996), p. 186.

6 Kant, *Correspondence*, p. 458.

7 Immanuel Kant, 'Observations on the Feeling of the Beautiful and Sublime', in *Immanuel Kant: Anthropology, History, and Education*,

ed. Günter Zöller and Robert B. Louden, trans. Paul Guyer (Cambridge, 2007), p. 61.

8 Immanuel Kant, 'Physical Geography' [1802], in *Immanuel Kant: Natural Science*, ed. Eric Watkins, trans. Olaf Reinhardt (Cambridge, 2012), p. 576. This quote moves in a dangerously explosive direction. Theorists such as Joseph Arthur de Gobineau (1816–1882) and Houston Stewart Chamberlain (1855–1927) – grandfathers of Nazism – developed theories with comparable racist hierarchies.

9 Immanuel Kant, 'Anthropology Friedländer 1775–1776', trans. G. Felicitas Munzel, in *Immanuel Kant: Lectures on Anthropology*, ed. Allen W. Wood and Robert B. Louden (Cambridge, 2012), p. 111.

10 Michael N. Forster, 'Introduction', in *Herder – Philosophical Writings*, trans. and ed. Michael N. Forster (Cambridge, 2002), p. xxxiii.

11 Rae Langton, 'Duty and Desolation', *Philosophy*, LXVII/262 (1992), p. 503.

12 Kant, 'Religion within the Boundaries of Mere Reason', p. 192.

13 Jean-Jacques Rousseau, *Emile; or, On Education*, trans. Allan Bloom (New York, 1979), p. 295.

14 Johann Gottfried Herder, 'Kant's Practical Philosophy: Herder's Lecture Notes', in *Immanuel Kant: Lecture on Ethics*, trans. Peter Heath (Cambridge, 1997), p. 34.

15 Kant, 'Anthropology from a Pragmatic Point of View', in *Immanuel Kant, Anthropology, History, and Education*, ed. Zöller and Louden, p. 312n.

16 Kant, 'Religion within the Bounds of Mere Reason', p. 154.

17 Roland Barthes, *Mythologies* [1957] (New York, 1972), pp. 74–5.

18 G.W.F. Hegel, 'Who Thinks Abstractly?', in Walter Kaufman, *Hegel: Reinterpretation, Texts, and Commentary* (New York, 1965), p. 465.

19 James Beattie, 'Essay on the Nature and Immutability of Truth' [1770] in *Early Responses to Hume*, vol. II, ed. James Fieser (London, 2003), pp. 277–8.

20 For a well-argued presentation of this position, see Michael O. Hardimon, *Rethinking Race* (Cambridge, MA, 2017).

21 Ibid., p. 2.

22 E.A.Ch. Wasianski, 'Immanuel Kant in seinem letzten Lebensjahren' [1804], in *Immanuel Kant: Ein Lebensbild nach Darstellen der Zeitgenossen – Borowski, Jachmann, Wasianski*, ed. Hermann Schwarz (Halle, 1907), p. 334.

23 Ibid., trans. as 'The Last Days of Immanuel Kant' by Thomas de Quincey in *Last Days of Immanuel Kant and Other Writings* (Edinburgh, 1862), p. 166.

24 Reinhold Bernhard Jachmann, *Immanuel Kant geschildert in Briefen einen Freund* (Königsberg, 1804), p. 188.

25 John Rewald, 'Modern Fakes of Modern Pictures', *ArtNews*, LII/1 (March 1953), p. 18.

26 Uwe Schultz states, 'In 1950, Kant's sarcophagus, which was still undamaged under the rubble of the mausoleum, was secretly broken into and robbed by unknown perpetrators,' in *Kant* (Hamburg, 1965), p. 43.

Epilogue: Kant's Legacy

1 Frederick C. Beiser, *The Genesis of Neo-Kantianism, 1796–1880* (Oxford, 2014), p. 1.

2 John Donne, *The Complete Poetry and Selected Prose of John Donne*, ed. Charles M. Coffin (New York, 1994), p. 441.

3 Karl Marx, 'Contribution to the Critique of Hegel's *Philosophy of Right*: Introduction', in *The Marx-Engels Reader*, ed. Robert C. Tucker, 2nd edn (New York, 1978), p. 60.

4 Martin Heidegger, *Being and Time*, trans. John Macquarrie and Edward Robinson (New York, 1962), pp. 191, 191–2.

5 Benjamin Lee Whorf, *Language, Thought, and Reality: Selected Writings of Benjamin Lee Whorf*, ed. John B. Carroll (Cambridge, MA, 1956), pp. 213–14.

Select Bibliography

Beiser, Frederick C., *The Fate of Reason: German Philosophy from Kant to Fichte* (Cambridge, MA, 1987)

—, *The Genesis of Neo-Kantianism, 1796–1880* (Oxford, 2014)

Cassirer, Ernst, *Kant's Life and Thought*, trans. James Haden (New Haven, CT, and London, 1981)

De Quincey, Thomas, *Last Days of Immanuel Kant and Other Writings* (Edinburgh, 1871)

Gardner, Sebastian, *Routledge Philosophy GuideBook to Kant and the 'Critique of Pure Reason'* (Abingdon, 1999)

Gulyga, Arsenij, *Immanuel Kant: His Life and Thought*, trans. Marijan Despalatović (Boston, MA, 1987)

Guyer, Paul, *Kant* (Abingdon, 2006)

—, *Kant and the Claims of Taste* (Cambridge, 1979)

—, *Kant's Impact on Moral Philosophy* (Oxford, 2024)

Kant, Immanuel, 'Anthropology from a Pragmatic Point of View [1798]', trans. Robert B. Louden, in *Immanuel Kant: Anthropology, History, and Education*, ed. and trans. Günter Zöller and Robert B. Louden (Cambridge, 2007), pp. 227–429

—, *Critique of the Power of Judgment*, ed. Paul Guyer, trans. Paul Guyer and Eric Matthews (Cambridge, 2000)

—, 'Critique of Practical Reason [1788]', trans. Mary J. Gregor, in *Immanuel Kant: Practical Philosophy*, ed. Mary J. Gregor (Cambridge, 1996), pp. 133–272

—, *Critique of Pure Reason*, trans. Paul Guyer and Allen W. Wood (Cambridge, 1998)

—, 'Groundwork of the Metaphysics of Morals [1785]', in *Immanuel Kant: Practical Philosophy*, ed. Mary J. Gregor (Cambridge, 1996), pp. 37–108

—, 'The Metaphysics of Morals [1797]', in *Immanuel Kant: Practical Philosophy*, ed. Mary J. Gregor (Cambridge, 1996), pp. 353–604

—, *Observations on the Feeling of the Beautiful and Sublime*, ed. Patrick Frierson and Paul Guyer (Cambridge, 2011)

— 'Prolegomena to Any Future Metaphysics that Will Be Able to Come Forward as Science', trans. Gary Hatfield, in *Immanuel Kant: Theoretical Philosophy After 1781*, ed. Henry Allison and Peter Heath (Cambridge, 2002), pp. 29–170

— 'Religion within the Boundaries of Mere Reason [1793]', trans. George di Giovanni, in *Immanuel Kant: Religion and Natural Theology*, trans. and ed. Allen W. Wood and George di Giovanni (Cambridge, 1996), pp. 39–216

Klinke, Willibald, *Kant for Everyman*, trans. Michael Bullock (London, 1951)

Kuehn, Manfred, *Kant: A Biography* (Cambridge, 2001)

Naragon, Steve, 'Kant in the Classroom', https://users.manchester.edu/Facstaff/SSNaragon/Kant/Home/index.htm

Stuckenberg, J.H.W., *The Life of Immanuel Kant* (London, 1882)

Wenley, R. M., *Kant and His Philosophical Revolution* (Edinburgh, 1910)

Wicks, Robert, *Routledge Philosophy GuideBook to Kant on Judgment* (Abingdon, 2007)

Wood, Allen W., *Kantian Ethics* (Cambridge, 2007)

—, *Kant and Religion* (Cambridge, 2020)

Acknowledgements

I owe a great debt to the many philosophers and historians who have devoted their time and, in some instances, the bulk of their academic careers to the study of Kant and his philosophy. Without their work, this book would have been impossible to write. Invaluable in this regard has been the work of Steve Naragon, whose extensive research on Kant stands as nothing less than a treasure for anyone interested in the details of Kant's life and times. Manfred Kuehn's monumental biography of Kant was also crucial for closing some of the gaps. I read his book many years ago with enormous appreciation but decided to reread and consult it only after having finished a draft of the present work, lest it interfere with the development of my own estimation of Kant. These two scholars deserve endless thanks for their devotion to one of history's great philosophers.

The writings of others have influenced the thoughts and details contained herein. Having stood upon their shoulders, I would like to acknowledge the following individuals: Frederick C. Beiser, William H. Carter, Alix Cohen, David Neave, Paul Guyer, Gerfried Horst, Anja Jauernig, Reidar Maliks, Nicole Pohl, Isabel Schnabel, Hyun Song Shin, Jill Storm, John Tilley, Simon Wain-Hobson, Owen Ware, Paul Warren, Eric Watkins, Kenneth R. Westphal, Allen W. Wood, John H. Zammito and Günter Zöller.

At the University of Auckland, I would also like to thank Professor Kim Phillips, Head of the School of Humanities, for her unwavering support and enthusiasm for this project, as well as the Faculty of Arts, through whose generosity I received a valuable period of research leave to assist in completing the manuscript.

Two of my early teachers of Kant deserve special recognition, to whom I gratefully dedicate this book: Charles McCracken (1933–2020), an expert in the philosophies of George Berkeley and Nicolas Malebranche, and Donald W. Crawford (1938–2022), a pioneer in the study of Kant's aesthetics and lover of natural beauty.

Photo Acknowledgements

The author and publishers wish to express their thanks to the sources listed below for illustrative material and/or permission to reproduce it. Some locations of artworks are also given below, in the interest of brevity:

AdobeStock: p. 177 (vodolej); Alamy: pp. 19 (Dmitrii Melnikov), 62 (The Granger Collection), 165 (Science History Images), 173 (Heritage Image Partnership Ltd); Château de Versailles: p. 40 (right); © CJP 2026, all rights reserved/www.cjpart.co.uk: p. 60; collection of the author: p. 92; Frankfurter Goethe-Haus: p. 126 (left); Gleimhaus – Museum der deutschen Aufklärung, Halberstadt: p. 105 (right); Herzog Anton Ulrich-Museum, Braunschweig: p. 40 (left); Herzog August Bibliothek, Wolfenbüttel (CC BY-SA 3.0 DE): pp. 105 (left), 127; Münchner Stadtmuseum: p. 140; Musée d'art et d'histoire, Geneva: p. 70; Museum Stadt Königsberg: pp. 157, 158; Nationalmuseum, Stockholm: p. 66; National Portrait Gallery, Smithsonian Institution, Washington, DC: p. 35; The New York Public Library: p. 13; Rijksmuseum, Amsterdam: pp. 23, 126 (right), 155; Schiller-Nationalmuseum und Deutsches Literaturarchiv, Marbach am Neckar: p. 78; Technische Universiteit Delft: p. 98; Universität Leipzig: p. 84 (right); Universitätsbibliothek Johann Christian Senckenberg, Frankfurt am Main: p. 169; Wikimedia Commons: pp. 6 (Hamburger Kunsthalle, photo An-d, CC BY-SA 3.0), 18 (Königsberger Dom; photo Zairon, CC BY-SA 4.0), 84 (left; Jüdisches Museum, Berlin, photo W.pseudon, CC BY-SA 4.0), 110 (public domain), 160 (photo GIC198, CC BY-SA 4.0).